Surviving your
social work placement

Surviving your social work placement

Robert Lomax
Karen Jones
Sarah Leigh
Chris Gay

palgrave
macmillan

First published 2010 by
PALGRAVE MACMILLAN

Palgrave Macmillan in the UK is an imprint of
Macmillan Publishers Limited, registered in England,
company number 785998, of Houndmills, Basingstoke,
Hampshire RG21 6XS.

Palgrave Macmillan in the US is a division of St Martin's Press
LLC, 175 Fifth Avenue, New York, NY 10010.

Palgrave Macmillan is the global academic imprint of the
above companies and has companies and representatives
throughout the world.

Palgrave® and Macmillan® are registered trademarks in
the United States, the United Kingdom, Europe and other
countries

ISBN 978-0-230-22189-5

This book is printed on paper suitable for recycling and made
from fully managed and sustained forest sources. Logging,
pulping and manufacturing processes are expected to
conform to the environmental regulations of the country of
origin.

A catalogue record for this book is available from the British
Library.

A catalog record for this book is available from the Library of
Congress.

10 9 8 7 6 5 4 3 2 1
19 18 17 16 15 14 13 12 11 10

Printed in China

Brief contents

Full contents

Exercises

Figures and tables

Figures

Tables

Acknowledgements

Thanks to all the social work students and newly qualified social workers who contributed their ideas to this book.

Thanks also to our colleagues who offered guidance and support, along with our editors at Palgrave, Catherine Gray and Kate Llewellyn.

We'd also like to thank our families for their patience and encouragement, especially Sophie, Effie and Isaac Lomax; Hannah and Emily Greenslade; Oliver and Catherine Bennett; and Pamela Leigh.

The authors and publishers wish to thank the following for permission to use copyright material: Sage Publications, London, Los Angeles, New Delhi and Singapore, for permission to reproduce the 'Race's Ripple Model' from P. Race, *Making Learning Happen* (© Race, 2005); Pearson Education Inc. for permission to reproduce 'Kolb's Learning Cycle' from D. Kolb, *Experiential Learning: Experience as the Source of Learning*, © 1984, p. 21 (adapted with permission of Pearson Education, Inc., Upper Saddle River, NJ); Palgrave Macmillan for permission to reproduce 'Critical Incident Analysis Technique' from A. Beverley and A. Worsley, *Learning and Teaching in Social Work Practice* © 2007; Skills for Care and Development for permission to reproduce the *National Occupational Standards for Social Work* in Appendix A and the Scottish Executive and Scottish Government for permission to reproduce *Standards in Social Work Education (Scotland)* in Appendix B. Every effort has been made to trace the copyright holders, but if any have been inadvertently overlooked the publishers will be pleased to make the necessary arrangements at the first opportunity.

Meet the author team

Robert Lomax is a Staff Tutor at the Faculty of Health and Social Care at the Open University. He has fifteen years' experience of working in community mental health services and continues to practise as a social worker.

Karen Jones is a Principal Lecturer in social work at the University of the West of England, Bristol. She has worked extensively as a social worker and practice educator and has researched and published on social work education and practice. She is joint editor of *Best Practice in Social Work: Critical Perspectives* (Palgrave, 2008).

Sarah Leigh is a Senior Lecturer at the University of the West of England. She has recently practised in Local Authority Children and Young People's Services, and has completed research and writing in this field. She teaches child protection as a specialist subject, and is a placement tutor for students at all levels of the degree programme.

Chris Gay has enjoyed a long career in social work as a practitioner and manager, working with students as their practice teacher and tutor. She currently works as a practice learning and post qualifying awards coordinator with South Gloucestershire Council.

Introduction

Welcome to your guide to surviving your social work placement. You will find that it is full of practical, effective advice and ideas designed not only to help you survive your placement, but to ensure that it is a really positive and useful experience.

For most social work students, practice placements are an exciting time. You probably embarked on a career in social work because you are interested in learning about and working with people and understand that not everyone can help themselves at every stage of their lives. It is also likely that your values lead you to want to make a difference to people's lives and to do what you can to help create a fairer society. Your placement is an opportunity to begin to put these interests and beliefs into action.

Who is this book for?

This is a book written first and foremost for students embarking on a social work placement, whether they are right at the beginning or near the end of their social work course. It will also be useful for students on a range of non-social work programmes including nursing, youth work, mental health and other areas of health and social care practice.

We have chosen to address *you* the student throughout and to place your experience as a learner at the heart of the book. However, the responsibility for a successful placement is not yours alone and many of the activities, ideas and advice contained here can be shared with your practice educator and others involved in your placement to help them to help you develop and progress. The book is also a useful resource for practice educators. Many of the discussion points and activities can be used as tools in supervision or as part of other guided learning activities and preparation for practice.

Why am I likely to find it useful?

This book contains lots of helpful ideas and practical advice to help you through the challenges and enable you to make the most of the opportunities you are offered on placement.

It is designed to complement and support your wider reading and learning and enable you to use this to demonstrate your competence in practice.

As a social work student in the UK you will be expected to show that you have met a set of occupational standards for social work (these vary slightly across the different countries of the UK and students in other countries will have different requirements to meet). The precise standards you need to demonstrate in any particular placement will also vary depending on what stage of your training you have reached. Whether this is your first or your final placement, there are many suggestions and activities in the chapters that follow, designed to help you to use and develop your knowledge in order to meet the relevant occupational standards and pass your placement.

The authors are all qualified social workers from a variety of practice backgrounds, currently working in universities or agency training departments. We each have many years' experience of supporting students during their placements and, above all, we share a commitment to high quality student-centred social work education and the promotion of best social work practice. In addition to our own experience we have drawn on the expertise of students and former students from across the UK. Throughout this book you will find the (anonymised) voices of students who shared with us their thoughts and experiences of being on placement. Students like Eve and Wilf (below) are able to offer insights and advice based on their own learning about what can really help you as a social work student to make the most of your placement.

> 66 I am pleased to give my feedback on 'The Survival Guide', and I welcome the idea. I needed help with using theory in practice – even though I had quite good academic marks I still struggled with the demands of placement.
>
> **Eve** *second-year student*

> 66 I just couldn't get the hang of writing in a reflective way. I had come from a very different world of commerce as a mature student and I just didn't get it. A book like this would definitely have helped me get the idea more quickly!
>
> **Wilf** *third-year student*

How can I make best use of the book?

The book is written so that you can dip in and out of it. Although the chapters are in a sequence that broadly follows the placement process, each one can also be read independently. The idea is to use different chapters as and when you need them rather than necessarily working through from beginning to end. Similarly, there are some sections which are particularly useful if you are just beginning your first placement and others which you may not use until you reach your second or third placement. It is a book you can usefully pick up and read even if you only have half an hour to spare on the bus, the train or in your lunch break. At the same time, it is important to do more than just read the book – you need to *use* it. Each chapter includes exercises and activities to provoke ideas and deepen your understanding of the issues involved in social work practice. There are also suggestions about further reading or web-based resources you can use to follow up the ideas presented in greater depth at the end of chapters.

Chapter 1, *Getting started,* takes you through the placement finding process into your first few days and the early stages of your induction. There are lots of friendly tips and advice about what to expect and how to make sure that you prepare as well as possible for the start of your placement.

Chapter 2, *Learning for practice,* helps you to think about the knowledge and skills that you bring to your placement as well as what you need to learn and how to make sure that these are reflected in your 'learning agreement'. There is a strong focus on reflection as a tool for making sense of practice and opportunities to understand the ways you learn best and how to make the most of these.

Chapter 3, *Using theory and knowledge in practice,* seeks to demystify theoretical knowledge and gives you a framework for applying theory to practice. The image of a jigsaw puzzle is used to show how you can bring together the different forms of knowledge that underpin social work practice as a coherent whole.

Chapter 4, *Keeping service users central to your learning and practice,* provides several theoretical models and a number of practical exercises designed to ensure that the individuals, families and communities with whom you are working remain at the heart of your learning and your future practice. Service user feedback in its many different forms is explored as an important aspect of learning and assessment.

Chapter 5, *Making the most of supervision,* helps you to understand what you can expect from supervision sessions and how to make the most of them. The chapter looks at some of the challenges and issues that can arise in the supervisory relationship and how you can help to resolve them, as well as other ways in which you can be an active and engaged supervisee.

Chapter 6, *Being assessed,* includes lots of ideas about ways in which you can ensure that your hard work on placement is visible and recognised. Few people enjoy being assessed, but this chapter will enable you to look at assessment as an important step on the road to becoming a competent, qualified practitioner.

Chapter 7, *Managing stress on placement,* recognises that placements can be stressful and difficult and that you may not always find it easy to cope with the practical and emotional demands you may face. The chapter offers lots of helpful and realistic solutions to enable you to recognise, avoid and deal with stress.

Chapter 8, *Troubleshooting,* guides you through some of the difficulties that can occur during your placement and illustrates them with real practice examples. A model of problem solving is introduced to enable you to work through challenges that arise on placement as constructively as you can.

Chapter 9, *Moving on from your placement,* looks at ways of ensuring that the end of your placement is a positive experience for everyone involved. Whether you are returning to university or embarking on your first qualified social work job, there are ideas about how to build on your learning and continue your development as an increasingly skilled and confident practitioner.

A word about terminology

The language of social work practice and education changes often and sometimes differs between areas, courses and certainly between countries. We have done our best to use the most widely understood terms, but even so, some of these may be less familiar to some readers than to others.

The word 'placement' occurs throughout the book as this tends to be widely used by students and others in general conversation, even though the more formal 'practice learning opportunity' is increasingly common in the UK. We have tended to write about 'university' as this is now where the great majority of social work training takes place in the UK, although we recognise that some courses are based in colleges of Further Education. The term 'practice educator' is used to describe the person responsible for your learning and assessment on placement, although in some places this person may be known as the practice assessor or field educator. Some placements involve a 'supervisor' who also has a distinct role, so this term is also used where appropriate.

Finally ...

We wish you every success with your placement, with your social work course and with your future career and we hope that this book will play a part in helping you to achieve that success.

The final words of this introduction go to Sara, a recent social work graduate:

> So many people in the world never get the chance to study. I say grab the opportunity. Studying is always a bit of pleasure and quite a lot of pain. Yes, placements were demanding but they're the 'real thing'. It's been worth it for me. I have a good team in my first job. I have to say frankly that it changed my life – it's the best thing I have ever done.
>
> SARA *newly qualified social worker*

Further reading and resources

S. Thompson and N. Thompson, *The Critically Reflective Practitioner* (Basingstoke: Palgrave Macmillan, 2008). Chapter 1 'What Is Reflective Practice?' gives helpful case studies and quotations from social workers about how critical reflection helped them to practise well.

1 Getting started

This chapter will help you to ...

- **Understand the important role of placements in social work training**
- **Prepare for your placement**
- **Manage your first contact with the placement agency**
- **Get started on your placement**

" You need to find a placement to meet your learning needs – I didn't really engage in the process early enough – try to open a dialogue with the University about what you want to get out of it – You won't always get what you want, but you will then start thinking about it.

JODIE *second-year student*

" You do need to get yourself organised as being in practice and being assessed can be pretty demanding. I would say to any new student getting ready for placement – get your home life sorted as far as possible.

DOMINIC *third-year student*

Most social work courses start with university-based learning. The opportunity to try out the theories, skills and methods you have read about and practised in the classroom is an exciting prospect, but it can also be a daunting one. This chapter aims to help you make the most of your placement by being as well prepared as you can be. One of the most important ways of doing this is to take the advice of the students quoted above and plan ahead. We will make some suggestions about how to achieve this as well as providing tips, practical advice, exercises and information about how to ensure that the beginning of your placement is an enjoyable and effective learning experience.

The role of placements in social work training

Placements are at the heart of social work training. On some courses learning in practice is about half of all learning that takes place. Social work students are also required to have experience:

- in at least two practice settings *and*
- of providing services to at least two user groups.

A set of National Occupational Standards (Standards in Social Work Education, in Scotland), including a statement of values and ethics, provide the criteria by which social work students are assessed in practice. The UK standards are reproduced as appendices A and B in this book; you can also read more about them in Chapter 6, *Being assessed.* Most non-UK countries have their own

standards and requirements by which students on placement are assessed.

Your experience of being on placement and the way in which you prepare for it will therefore vary depending on the stage of training you have reached and the standards and requirements you are expected to meet. You will learn a great deal from your first placement, which you will carry to your second (and in some cases third or fourth) placement. The expectations of those involved in your practice education, the requirements of your university course and the expectations you have of yourself will also increase as you become more knowledgeable, competent and experienced. By the time you complete your final placement, those involved in assessing your practice will be expecting you to show that you can practise in the way that would be expected of a newly qualified social worker.

At all levels, placements are an opportunity to put your academic learning into practice and to find out more about the knowledge, skills and values needed to work safely and effectively with different groups of service users. If you are reading this book as a student thinking about your first placement, the prospect of being a fully qualified and competent social worker may feel a long way off. It is important to remember, however, that the purpose of your learning on placement and at university is all about becoming a skilled and confident professional practitioner. Ensuring that you make the most of each placement by preparing well and getting off to a good start is an essential building block along the road to achieving this goal.

Preparing for placement

Organising the placement

The process of identifying and organising placements is usually the responsibility of social work course providers rather than individual students. The precise way this works will differ from university to university. It will almost certainly depend on the structure of your course, the availability of placements in your area and the way in which responsibility for arranging them is organised between the university and practice agencies. Other considerations will include the stage you have reached in your training and the sorts of formal national requirements outlined above. This can mean that for reasons beyond the control of your university, the amount of choice you have over where your placement takes place is limited. However, if you are given an opportunity to negotiate your placement setting, you should take the advice of Jodie, the student quoted at the beginning of this chapter, and seize it!

This book is all about being an active participant in your placement experience and, where possible, this should start before your placement begins. Some of the ways in which you may be able to play an active role in the process of identifying a placement include:

- Finding out about the procedure for organising placements. Understanding the time scales and responsibilities involved will help to ensure that you make a useful contribution rather than hindering the process.
- Filling in any forms you are given about your preferences, previous experience and learning needs as fully as possible – this information may be used to match you to a particular placement.
- Talking to your tutor about the sort of placement you feel you need. Staff on social work courses are generally very experienced in assessing the learning needs of students. Your tutor may therefore have a different idea from you about the placement that would suit you best.
- Being honest with yourself and with those involved in organising your placement. Exaggerating your past experience or ignoring particular learning needs will not help you to pass your placement *or* to become a good social worker.

Exercise 1.1 is designed to help you reflect honestly on the sort of learning you need from your placement. It will help you to think about the importance of learning in and from practice and may also help in the process of identifying a suitable placement. If you are preparing for your first placement, it might be tempting to answer that you need to know 'everything' or perhaps that you don't yet know what you need to learn. The examples come from first-year students and should help you to be more specific, but take care to apply them to your *own* particular learning needs.

- What **knowledge** do I need to develop during this placement?

  Example: *I've learnt quite a bit about the idea of evidence-based practice, but I'd like the chance to get to know some of the up-to-date research in relation to a particular setting or service user group and see how it actually relates to practice. I've also enjoyed learning about the law underpinning social work, but I can't really understand the way specific legislation impacts on the day-to-day job of social work; I need to know much more about this.*

  Your learning needs …

- What **skills** do I need to develop and learn?

  Example: *I feel like all I know is the theory of how to talk to people as a social worker. I've done loads of role plays, but I haven't got much actual experience of practice. I'm not very confident and I'll really need to develop my communication skills, whatever setting I end up in.*

  Your learning needs …

- What **social work values** do I need to develop?

  Example: *I've read about anti-oppressive practice and I feel very committed to it, but I don't understand how it fits with the procedures and regulations that social workers have to work within. I want to get a better understanding of what social work values actually mean in practice.*

Your learning needs …

In addition to thinking about your learning needs on placement, it is important to reflect on your existing skills and experience – in other words, all the things you will *bring* to the placement. Chapter 2, *Learning for practice*, includes exercises to be used during your placement to help you think about the strengths you already have; you may also find it helpful to complete these as part of the process of finding the right placement for you.

Waiting to hear about your placement

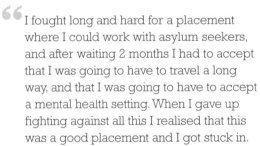

I fought long and hard for a placement where I could work with asylum seekers, and after waiting 2 months I had to accept that I was going to have to travel a long way, and that I was going to have to accept a mental health setting. When I gave up fighting against all this I realised that this was a good placement and I got stuck in.

SAMERA *second-year student*

You may know well in advance exactly where your placement is going to be. If this is the case, you will be able to do plenty of background reading and prepare thoroughly for the experience. Unfortunately however, it is sometimes not possible to let students know where they are going to be placed until shortly before the placement begins.

It may even be that you start your placement late. If this happens to you, try not to worry – it is very unlikely that your placement will be delayed for more than a short time. Whatever your situation, there are lots of things you can do while you are waiting to hear, which will ensure that you get off to a good start once your placement begins. Box A identifies some of these.

Box A	Making use of the time before placement starts

- Get your notes from university in order and make sure you will be able to find any materials you might need to refer to during your placement.
- Read whatever placement guidance you have been given by your university and make sure you know what is expected of you when you start your placement.
- If you are going to be starting a second or third placement, remind yourself what you learnt on your first placement and think about how you can build on this.
- If you haven't already done so, complete Exercise 1.1 to help you think about your learning priorities.
- Think about your home and family life and whether there are plans you can make in advance to ensure that your placement can be managed alongside the rest of your life.

Planning to begin your placement

" I was quite anxious about my placement, so I went to talk to my tutor about it. She was really good at helping me get it in perspective and realise that I didn't need to know everything before I started.

ELLEN *second-year student*

" I tried driving to and from my placement at different times of the day before I started. I needed an idea of idea of how long it would take me because sometimes I had to get to school to pick the children up.

WILF *third-year student*

Once you know where your placement is going to be and when it is going to begin, you can start planning for it in much more detail. This might include some really practical steps such as the one described here by Wilf. Alternatively, it may be more about finding ways of dealing with the psychological impact of beginning a new placement, such as Ellen talks about. Being well prepared for your placement in every way will help to reduce stress and enable you to direct your energy into successful practice learning.

Good planning is also an essential social work skill. Pamela Trevithick (2005: 144) suggests two ways of thinking about planning for social work practice:

1 A reflective approach.
2 A checklist approach.

These two approaches are equally applicable to planning the beginning of your placement and complement each other in ensuring that you have thought deeply enough about what it means to begin a new placement (reflective approach) and that all the practicalities are covered (checklist approach). We have adapted Trevithick's approaches in the next two exercises.

The questions below will help you to reflect on your thoughts and feelings about starting placement and begin to plan in advance how best to manage these.

- How do I feel about the prospect of beginning this placement?

- What am I most anxious about?

- Why am I anxious and what can I do to address my anxiety?

- How have I managed similar anxieties in the past?

- What do I feel confident about?

- What can I do to make the most of the things I feel confident about?

The checklist below contains some suggestions about areas you need to think about when planning to begin your placement. Your university, your placement agency and your fellow students will probably have additional suggestions about what should be included on your checklist.

Have you planned for?
☐ Family commitments
☐ Social life
☐ Looking after yourself
☐ Journey to and from placement
☐ Finances
☐ Keeping in touch with fellow students
☐ Study time

What else do you need to do?

Home and family life

The exercises above included various reminders about the importance of planning your home and family life in preparation for your placement. This is an important aspect of the placement experience and worth considering in a little more depth. Many people find that undertaking their professional social work training presents quite a challenge for those closest to them. You may be very focused on your studies and on your development as a professional social worker, but you will probably also be changing as an individual. Most students find that taking time to talk with their families about the ideas they are studying and how this

Making contact with your placement for the first time

" I have been so busy since qualifying three years ago – just getting to grips with the job itself, but I used to love theory on my social work course and I know I need to read more. I am really looking forward to having a student and getting challenged again and having to read textbooks again.

CAMILLE *Child Care Social Worker*

is affecting them personally helps to ensure that family members are as understanding and supportive as possible.

You will probably find that your social work training has more of a practical impact on your family during your placements than at any other time. This will obviously depend on your individual circumstances. However, social work students with caring commitments need to plan particularly carefully in order to accommodate the impact of the placement on their home lives. The extent to which there is any flexibility in relation to working hours will depend on the requirements of both your course and your placement agency. This is something to explore with your university as part of the placement finding process. Some of the questions you might ask are:

- Is it possible to do the placement part time if I need to?
- How flexible are the hours – can I start early and finish early?
- Do I have to do any evening or weekend work?
- What happens if one of my family is ill?

It is worth remembering that agencies often really enjoy having students working with them, as Camille says. You will bring a fresh perspective to the team's work as well as knowledge and skills that will be useful to your colleagues.

Making contact with your placement before you actually start will help you to be well prepared and should mean that you feel less anxious about your first day. Your initial contact will usually be through a pre-placement visit. Sometimes the pre-placement visit can be an opportunity for you to decide whether you want to accept a particular placement. It can also give the agency a chance to decide whether you are the right student for them. You need to be clear in advance about whether this is the purpose of the visit, as it will affect the way you present yourself and the sorts of questions you ask. In most cases, however, the pre-placement visit is simply an opportunity to introduce yourself and find out more about the work you will be doing.

Exercise 1.4 lists some of the questions you might want to ask during your pre-placement visit. You will probably have other questions arising from the planning exercises earlier in this chapter.

Exercise 1.4	Planning your pre-placement visit
Question	**Answer**
• What are the hours of work?	
• Are there other students in the agency and could I speak to them before I start?	
• What could I read before I start to help me prepare for this placement?	
• Do students have their own desk and phone?	
• Have you been given information about my disability/ specific learning needs?	
• How do students organise study time when working with the team?	
• Your question...	
• Your question...	
• Your question...	

Practice placements in your own agency

If you are being sponsored by your employer to undertake social work training, you may undertake your placement in your own team or agency. If this is the case, you will have to give some thought to how you can make the experience work for you. The fact that you continue to be a paid employee of your agency and/or they are paying your university fees places you in a different position from a student who is studying independently for their social work degree.

> 66 If you are going into your own team again as a student, it's hard to say I'm not going to do all the work, or all the same type of work, that I used to. But in reality that is what you have to do from day one.
>
> DOMINIC *third-year student*

It will be important for your team manager and colleagues to realise that your role has changed. The work you do on placement may be similar to that which you did before you started your training. However, the purpose of your practice now includes the development of your skills towards meeting the relevant occupational standards and becoming a professional social worker.

It is important to think about ways that you can feel different when you return to your agency as a social work student on placement. Exercise 1.5 offers some suggestions about ways you might start to establish this difference and enable your colleagues to appreciate your new role.

Exercise 1.5 Establishing your role as a social work student	
Suggestions …	**Your ideas …**
• Move to a part of the office where you haven't sat before	
• Ask your team manager or practice educator to let your colleagues know about your new role	
• Move to a quiet room for study periods	
• Offer to do a presentation at the team meeting about what you've been learning at university	

Getting started on your placement

Your first few days

During the first few days of your placement you may feel a range of emotions, from excitement and elation to anxiety and fear. Many students who say that they found placements to be the most enjoyable part of their social work training also confess that they did not always feel this during the first few weeks. Conversely, some students who report initial feelings of confidence and excitement are challenged by the realities of the placement experience.

> **Remember**
> ... it is completely usual to feel anxious during your first few days on placement.

Whatever your initial experience it is important to remember that your practice educator and hopefully your other colleagues will want you to do well on placement and feel that they are there to help you succeed. If you have a question, whether it is about your service users or simply where to find the kettle, it is usually best to ask. The more you engage with your colleagues and services users the more involved you will feel in the placement.

Exercise 1.6 is a reminder that you have faced new challenges in the past and that you have got to grips with them successfully.

Use the grid below to reflect on some past challenges and how you have met them. You can complete it on your own or use it as a basis for discussion with your practice educator, tutor or fellow students.

Exercise 1.6 Meeting new challenges		
New challenge	**How did I meet the challenge?**	**What did I learn?**
Example: Feeling very anxious on my first day at college	Introduced myself to people and asked lots of questions	I am often shy at first, but that's okay and I can adapt to new situations
Example: Joining the gym and feeling embarrassed because I wasn't as fit as everyone else	Asked for help from the instructors. Identified a couple of other "new" people, so we could support each other	If I am finding something difficult, other people probably feel the same
Your example ...		
Your example ...		

Getting to know the people involved in your placement

Your practice learning team

A successful placement is a shared experience. There is a great deal that you can do to help your placement go well. However, others have a responsibility for ensuring that you have a fair opportunity to learn what you need to know and to demonstrate your competence in practice. In most placement settings, there will be a small number of people who are closely involved in your practice learning; they are sometimes referred to as the 'practice learning team'. Your practice learning team may include a day-to-day supervisor as well as someone who is responsible for your learning and assessment in practice. In many settings these roles are combined in a single 'practice educator'. Your tutor or someone else from your university will probably also be involved in some way, although the role played by universities in practice learning varies from institution to institution.

You will read more about the practice learning team in the chapters that follow. Chapter 2, *Learning for practice*, in particular looks at the 'learning agreement' as the place where the roles and responsibilities of those involved in your placement are defined, while Chapter 6, *Being assessed*, explores different tasks in relation to the assessment of your practice. During your first few days, however, you will be just beginning to meet and build a relationship with those most closely involved in your placement and with others who may have a less central role.

Others involved in your learning

In addition to your practice learning team, there will be a wide range of other people involved in your placement experience. Some of them will help with your learning and day-to-day practice and some may contribute to the assessment of your work. You may find it helpful to use a 'knowledge map' to remind yourself of the names and roles of different people you meet during the first few days of your placement and of the connections between them. Exercise 1.7 shows you how you might do this. You will come across knowledge maps again in Chapter 2.

Induction

Within your first few days on placement you should begin the process of learning what you need to know to begin working in your particular placement setting. This is usually called 'induction'. The way in which the induction process is organised as well as its length and content will vary between placements. You may also find that in some agencies you are expected to make a lot of your own induction arrangements, while in others this will be done for you.

The sorts of things you might expect your induction to include are:

- **Welcome and introductions**. Teams welcome students in different ways. You might arrive at your desk, and find a new diary on it, new stationery and your own computer. Perhaps you will be welcomed at a team meeting. However, if your welcome is more low-key than this, don't worry. Just make a start and begin to settle in.

Below is an example of a knowledge map indicating the names and roles of people involved in a placement. Draw your own map and make a note of the people you meet during the early part of your placement. You can start with your immediate team, but you may want to expand it to show the many different professionals and support staff you will be working with during your placement and the connections between them.

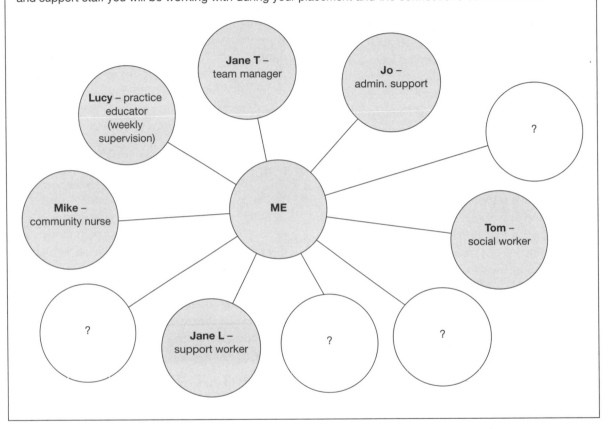

Introduce yourself to your new colleagues and begin to understand their roles.

- **Office procedures.** You will be told about the procedures for things like claiming expenses, using petty cash, and other day-to-day processes specific to your particular practice setting.

- **Health and safety.** You will probably receive some sort of health and safety training. This may include the way you are expected to indicate your whereabouts, such as procedures for signing in and out of the office and how to raise the alarm or call for help in an emergency.

- **Office property**. You may be given items belonging to the agency that are necessary to do the job, such as an office mobile phone, keys or 'swipe' cards, and identity badge. You may be required to sign for these and agree to their safe return.
- **Visits to other agencies.** These may be arranged for you or you might simply be provided with a list of contacts within local organisations and agencies. Visiting a range of organisations at an early stage will help you to build up a picture of the area and the type of work you will be doing.
- **Meeting other professionals**. Multi-agency and multi-professional practice are crucial dimensions of modern social work and core skills to be demonstrated in meeting the relevant occupational standards. It is therefore very important to begin to build good relationships early on. It will also help you to meet those key roles concerning multi-professional and inter-professional working.
- **Getting to know the locality**. This is particularly important if you are working in an agency which provides a service to people in the immediate neighbourhood. Twelvetrees (2002) advises workers to: 'Walk – don't ride.' That is, walk around the area in which you are working to find out what it might be like to live there. For example, are there steep hills which make it difficult for older people to get around? Is the street lighting poor, making crime more likely?

The next exercise suggests some other ways in which you might try to gain an understanding of the lives of the people you will be working with.

| **Exercise 1.8** | **Walk a mile in another person's shoes** |

The French sociologist Emile Durkheim (1858–1917) talked about the importance of seeing the world from different perspectives before making judgements about others (Durkheim 1983). The following activities and questions are intended to help you to see the world from the perspective of those you will be working with on placement. You may need to adapt it slightly to suit your particular placement.

If you are placed in an agency which works with local people:

- Make a list of all the voluntary and independent organisations in the area. Try to visit some of them.

  How easy is it to find out what is going on in the neighbourhood?

- Find out if there is a local newsletter

  What are the articles about? Do you think if you lived here it would be useful to you? Why?

- Talk to local people (e.g., in shops, doctors' surgeries, at bus stops)

  What do they think about services in their area?

If you are working with a particular service user group:

- Arrange to visit other agencies working with the same people

  What would it be like to use this youth club/homeless person's hostel/residential home etc.?

- How do people get to where they need to be? Try the forms of transport used by those you are working with.

  What would it be like to travel this way all the time?

Office culture – the things that are not written down

There are some things about getting to know a new work setting that are not written down anywhere and will probably not be part of your induction. It simply takes time to get to know how an organisation works and functions. You need to be patient in trying to understand it. Offices, teams and organisations all have their own culture and many of the informal 'dos and don'ts' are hard to appreciate when you first start. If there are things you don't know, this is probably because no one has thought to tell you rather than a deliberate attempt to exclude. The only way to find out about how the team *really works* is to observe and ask.

Finally ...

Beginning a new placement is challenging for even the most confident student, so you should not be surprised if you feel slightly anxious or overwhelmed in your first few days. Making use of the suggestions in this chapter will help you to get off to a good start by enabling you to:

- Plan ahead for your practice placement.
- Feel comfortable about meeting your new colleagues and settling into your work environment.

- Find ways of beginning to understand the experiences of the service users and carers with whom you will be working.

Further reading and resources

T. Lindsay and S. Orton, *Group Work Practice in Social Work* (Exeter: Learning Matters, 2008). Chapter 5 'Group Processes' will help you to understand some of the issues that working in a new team may present.

N. Thompson, *People Skills*, 3rd edition (Basingstoke: Palgrave Macmillan, 2009). Chapter 2 'Time Management' encourages you to look at using your time well, using your diary, and managing your own energy levels.

N. Thompson, *Understanding Social Work, – Preparing for Practice*, 3rd edition (Basingstoke: Palgrave Macmillan, 2009). This helpful and encouraging book will remind you of some of the basic skills needed to practise well and to begin your placement with confidence.

J. Walker, K. Crawford and J. Parker, *Practice Education in Social Work: A Handbook for Practice Teachers, Assessors and Educators* (Exeter: Learning Matters, 2008). This is written for practice educators, but it may also be useful for you to understand the context of placement.

2 Learning for practice

This chapter will help you to ...

- **Think about your learning strengths and needs**
- **Play an active part in negotiating your 'learning agreement'**
- **Take control of your learning**
- **Find out about different models of learning and identify your learning style**
- **Get to grips with reflection**
- **Identify some useful tools for learning**

---

66 You do find that you know things though – it's amazing how it begins to fall into place after a while. The things I'd read and learnt at university made a lot more sense when I was able to relate them to practice.

JODIE *second-year student*

66 I just felt like I knew absolutely nothing – I couldn't begin to see how all that stuff I'd learnt in college could be any use to me in the real world of practice. I felt completely out of my depth.

YASMIN *first-year student*

Starting a new social work placement is a great opportunity to put your learning from university into practice. The process of becoming a professional social worker involves acquiring a set of skills and knowledge that you can apply confidently in practice situations. Of course it is not unusual to feel out of your depth like Yasmin or to believe that none of what you have learned on your course is going to be of any use in the 'real world' of practice. In fact, like Jodie, you almost certainly know more than you think you do. You will also have people involved in your placement who are there specifically to help you make the connections between theory and practice and move further along the road towards becoming a skilled, competent social worker. This chapter will help to increase your confidence by identifying your strengths as well as the areas where you may need further support from practice educators, university tutors and others. It also offers useful tips on how to make the most of the learning available to you on placement.

Celebrating your strengths and acknowledging your learning needs

There is a lot to learn on any placement and this can feel overwhelming. However, it is as important to be aware of the talents, qualities and experiences you bring *to* the placement as the many things you need to learn *from* it. Being open with yourself (and with your supervisor) about your strengths *and* the things you need to learn will enable you to take advantage of the opportunities the placement provides.

Strengths and needs analysis

A good way of working out what knowledge you already have as well as the things you need to learn more about is a 'strengths and needs' analysis (see Exercise 2.1). This is a useful tool for helping you and your practice educator to identify some of the practice activities that will enable you to meet your particular learning needs.

Your 'strengths' list could include:

- ☑ Skills gained from past practice experience
- ☑ Knowledge from your college or university course
- ☑ Things you instinctively know you do well

Your 'learning needs' list could include:

- ☑ Areas or activities where you have little or no experience
- ☑ Activities that you find frightening or intimidating
- ☑ Areas where you feel you have little underpinning knowledge

List A shows one person's strengths and learning needs, but everyone's list will be different. *Your* list will depend on your unique experiences, interests and skills.

LIST A	
Strengths	**Learning needs**
☑ Listening skills	☑ Group work
☑ Knowledge of childcare law	☑ Talking to people with learning disabilities
☑ Showing empathy	
☑ Talking to children	☑ Mental Health Law

Exercise 2.1 **Strengths and learning needs**

1 Use the boxes below to list your **strengths** and your **learning needs**.

Strengths	Learning needs

2 Once you have completed your lists, use them to make a **Learning Action Plan**.

Learning Action Plan	
What opportunities are there to develop my strengths during this placement?	What do I need to do to make this happen?
What opportunities are there for my learning needs to be met during this placement?	What do I need to do to make this happen?

Using your Learning Action Plan

It may sound obvious, but once you have completed your analysis and your Learning Action Plan, it is important to make use of it rather than setting it to one side and forgetting about it.

Remember
... you are on placement to learn. No one will expect you to know every thing immediately.

You can do this by:

☑ Using it as a basis for your learning agreement and for discussion in supervision

☑ Using it in tutorials and other university-based, placement-related activities

☑ Writing about it in your reflective diary (you can read about reflective diaries later in this chapter)

☑ Revisiting and revising it at regular points in the placement

☑ Celebrating your growing list of *strengths* as the placement goes on!

Your learning agreement

Most placements in the UK will involve the completion of some sort of learning agreement. The learning agreement should be a place where you can celebrate your strengths, acknowledge your learning needs and begin to identify how these can be met. It should also clarify the ways in which the work you will be doing on placement will enable you to meet the relevant occupational standards or other specific requirements. The content and style of learning agreements varies from placement to placement and from university to university. However, the points below will give you an idea of some common themes, while the tips which follow should help you to get the most from your particular learning agreement.

- **What is a learning agreement?**
  A learning agreement or learning contract enables the negotiated and agreed expectations of those closely involved in the placement to be set down in writing. Although you will probably be expected to use some sort of pro forma, which incorporates standard questions, it is very important that your placement agreement is individualised and specific to *your* learning needs.
- **What will it cover?**
  The learning agreement will cover practicalities like the hours you are expected to work, how much study time you are entitled to and how you will be supervised. It is very helpful to ensure that these points are clarified at an early stage, so that misunderstandings can be avoided later on. Most learning agreements will also include something about the type and amount of work you will be expected to undertake. This should be linked to the occupational standards relevant to the placement, as well as to the assessment requirements of the university and to your own identified learning needs.
- **Who will be involved?**
  The completion of the learning agreement should always be a negotiated, collaborative process. The way in which it happens will vary according to the requirements and conventions of your particular course. A university tutor will probably sign your learning agreement along with those who are most closely involved in supervising and assessing your practice. This may be one, two or three people, depending on the way in which your placement is organised. What is important is that the agreement is used to establish a clear framework on which all the key participants are agreed.
- **When and how will the learning agreement be completed?**
  This will depend on the way in which your particular university course organises its placements. Sometimes learning agreements are completed before the placement begins and sometimes within the first few weeks. It is not a good idea to delay much more than this or you may find yourself undertaking work without a clear idea of what is expected of you. You may be asked to type up the final version of the learning agreement or someone else may take responsibility for this. Either way, it should be signed by everyone involved.
- **Why is it important?**
  Your learning agreement will help you to feel clear and confident about what you can reasonably expect from your placement and what is likely to be expected of you. The process of negotiating the learning agreement is an opportunity for you and your practice educator to ensure that your individual learning needs and the specific standards you are required to meet are matched as closely as possible to the opportunities the placement has to offer. Box A has some tips on how you can make the learning agreement work for you

---

Box A | Top tips for learning agreements

☑ **Bring the Learning Action Plan from your 'strengths and needs analysis' to your learning agreement meeting.** This will enable everyone involved to see that you have thought about what you have to offer and where you need to develop.

☑ **Be honest.** You are on placement to learn. The more open you can be about the areas of your practice you want and need to improve, the more likely it is that the placement will meet your needs.

☑ **Make sure the learning agreement is a 'living' document.** It is important that the learning agreement doesn't simply get filed away once it has been completed. Your learning needs will evolve as the placement progresses and you begin to demonstrate different skills and areas of competence. Be proactive in bringing it to supervision and negotiating revisions to its content.

Taking control of your learning

❝ My practice educator and my university tutor were both very helpful. They gave me lots of ideas about what to read and how to find relevant research. In the end, though, I realised it was also important for me to ask the questions I needed to ask and find reading for myself about things I didn't understand.

NAS *third-year student*

As Nas suggests, you will get more from your placement if you can take some control of your own learning. Your practice educator and others are

there to help you, but if you are proactive in your approach, they will be better able to do this.

The learning you experience on placement will take many different forms and will relate to social work practice in a variety of ways. Some of the knowledge you acquire will be quite general. For example, you will learn more about organisations and teams and you will probably improve your skills in other areas such as record keeping and report writing. Other learning will relate specifically to your practice on placement and is likely to involve drawing on evidence from theory and research, as well as expertise gained from your own and others' experience. You can read much more about different kinds of knowledge for practice in Chapter 3, *Using theory and knowledge in practice*. The rest of this chapter looks at some of the skills and techniques you can use to get to grips with the wealth of information and potential learning that a new social work placement represents.

The suggestions below and the tips that follow each main point are based on the experiences of students who have been through the placement process; you can probably add your own ideas.

Watch what's going on around you

It doesn't matter whether your placement is in an office, a residential home, a community setting or somewhere else. Watch how others work and give yourself permission to absorb what's going on. Some things that might help you to make the most of your observations are:

• Don't worry about looking as though you're not doing anything – watching is an important activity and a good way to learn.

- Try to think *critically* about what is going on around you. Consider *how* and *why* rather than just *what* team members are doing and allow yourself to question what you see.
- Make a note of the things that you find difficult or puzzling as well as the methods and approaches that impress you.
- Use your notes to raise issues in supervision and to help you write your reflective diary (you can read about reflective diaries below and in Chapter 5, *Making the most of supervision*).

Ask questions and talk to people

Asking questions is another of the ways in which you can be proactive about your learning. Of course it's important to be sensitive about people's workloads and other priorities when you do this, but most social workers and other professionals will welcome the opportunity to talk about their practice. Important points to remember about this are:

- Check that people have time to talk before you engage them in a long conversation. It may be better to arrange a more convenient time to talk.
- If you do feel you've got more questions than you can reasonably ask, write them down and add them to a list of things to raise in supervision.
- Talk to a range of different professionals. 'Multi-professional' or 'multi-disciplinary' working is a key element of modern social work practice and people from other professions may well be involved in aspects of your learning and assessment on placement. Other professionals will have different roles from social workers and probably some shared and some different perspectives. Talking to them about what they do and the ways in which they collaborate with social workers will help you to understand how professionals can work together for the benefit of service users.
- Talk to service users. Finding out why people use a particular service and what they think of it will enable you to develop a more rounded critical perspective on the work you are doing.

Read as widely as you can

You can learn a great deal on placement by watching and listening to others; however, this will never be enough in itself to ensure that you have the knowledge, skills and understanding to be a fully competent, independent social work practitioner. It is important that your practice is also based on good evidence from up-to-date research and published writing about what constitutes the most relevant knowledge for practice. Some of the ways in which you might gather relevant reading materials include:

- Looking at what is available in your office. Most teams will have a stock of books, journals and other policy and practice documents.
- Check whether your agency has a library or a web-based resource containing useful materials for practice. The agency may have a nominated person you can contact, who has special responsibility for 'evidence' or 'knowledge' for practice.
- Ask which books, chapters, articles and websites team members have found useful. Some teams will be much more 'research minded' than others, but many people will at least have a favourite piece of reading or electronic resource to direct you to.
- Go back to your university notes and previous reading. The knowledge and skills you already have about theories, research and other evidence for practice are the bedrock that will enable you to practise confidently and effectively on placement. At the same time, your growing practice knowledge will help you to make more sense of what you are reading the second time round. You may also find it useful to look at Chapter 3, *Using theory and knowledge in practice*, where there are many more tips on how to apply theory to practice.
- Use your university library. Even if your placement is some distance away, you will be able to access the many on-line databases and other sources of knowledge that all universities now offer. Social work practitioners are increasingly expected to show that their work is thoroughly

evidence based. This is particularly important for you as a beginning practitioner. As you will already know, there is a wealth of research and other writing on best practice in social work. Your placement is an opportunity to really make practical use of this. Your practice educator will be able to guide you to relevant reading, but developing independent skills in finding materials for yourself is an important skill in the toolbox of the competent professional social worker.

- Read any notes and guidance you have been given about what is expected of you on placement very carefully. This is particularly important in relation to written assignments and portfolios, which may take a rather different form from the academic writing you have produced so far. If you are at all unsure of what is being asked for by your university, get in touch with your tutor or other relevant contact person.

Make good use of your study time

Finding time for independent study will probably be more difficult during your placement than at any other point in your course. This means that you need to make the best possible use of the periods of study you do have available. The key to this is *careful planning*. The points below will help you to make the best possible use of your study time:

- Spend time making sure that your course notes and assignments are ordered and accessible; highlight areas that are particularly relevant to your placement.
- Review your skills in accessing electronic databases and other resources. If you think you need support in this area, make a plan for how you can achieve it. You could, for example, ask a fellow student, tutor or librarian for help or arrange to attend a relevant workshop.
- Think about when and where you learn best. Some people work most effectively at home; others prefer the library. Some can concentrate better in the mornings, others in the evening. If you are a 'morning person' it may be best to collect books from the library in the evening and dedicate the morning to activities which need you to be more focused and alert, such as reading and writing.
- Be clear about what you can realistically achieve in the study period you have available and plan in advance the proportion of time you are going to spend on different activities.

Remember ... you will get more out of your placement if you take as much responsibility as you can for your own learning.

Exercise 2.2 How do you study?

Use the prompts below to plan your approach to studying. Your answers will help you to make a study timetable for placement.

Start by thinking about your preferred ways of studying:

- *When* do I study most effectively?

- *Where* do I study best?

- *What else* helps me to study well?

Then think about how you will fit these preferences into a realistic pattern of studying during your placement:

- What time do I have available for study during my placement?

- How can I use this most effectively?

- What else can I do to make sure I make best use of the time I have available?

- Try to avoid distractions and other commitments. You may think you can cook a meal, watch TV or sit in a café while you are studying, but if you are going to make the most of precious study time, you probably need to prioritise this and nothing else.

- Studying and preparing for assessment will almost certainly impact on your home and personal life while you are on placement. Nevertheless, it is important to make sure you take *some* time off. Looking after yourself and recharging your batteries is essential to your learning and to ensuring that your placement is a positive experience.

Models of learning

There are many different *models* of learning which try to explain how learning happens or the particular ways in which individuals learn. This section introduces some of the most popular models and looks at the ways in which these may be useful to you during your placement.

Honey and Mumford's learning styles

A great deal has been written about *learning styles*. A quick internet search will reveal some of the many different ideas there are on this topic. Perhaps the most useful thing to hold on to, however, is the fact that you will have your own style of learning and this may be different from the way your supervisor or many of your fellow students learn.

One of the most popular approaches to learning styles was devised by Peter Honey and Alan

Mumford (1986). You can download the full updated learning styles questionnaire on a pay-as-you-go basis from the internet, but a quick look at the four styles they identify may be enough to enable you to better understand your own approach to learning:

Reflectors ... are people who like to stand back, collect information and think about things before they reach a conclusion. They usually prefer to listen to the views of others before contributing their own ideas and don't like being rushed or put on the spot.

Theorists ... tend to be analytical and like to think problems through step by step. They enjoy complicated situations where they need to use knowledge and skills, but they are less keen on circumstances where feelings and emotions are involved.

Activists ... are enthusiastic about new experiences and new learning. They often take the lead in groups and like making decisions. They are not so comfortable working alone or in situations where they have to absorb and understand complicated information.

Pragmatists ... are practical and down to earth. They like to see the relevance of what they are learning and tend not to be very interested in theory and background information that has no obvious immediate benefit.

Exercise 2.3   What is your learning style?

Use the boxes below to describe your learning style and identify the learning you enjoy most and that which you like least. Then try to identify ways in which knowing this might help you during your placement.

I would describe my learning style as …

The kind of learning I like best is …	The kind of learning I like least is …

Knowing this will help me to …	Knowing this will help me to …

Identifying *your* learning style

In practice, of course, most people do not fit neatly into a single learning style category. You may feel that you are a mixture of two, three or all four learning styles or you might identify strongly with one learning style and to a lesser extent with another (a reflector with theorist tendencies or an activist with a touch of pragmatism, perhaps). Knowing how you learn best does not mean that you can avoid situations that do not provide your ideal learning environment. It might, however, help you to understand why you struggle more in some situations than others and enable you to take advantage of the learning opportunities from which you are most likely to benefit.

Race's ripples

Phil Race (1993, 1995) sees learning as ripples on a pond – each moving into the next (see Figure 2.1). His model relates particularly to learning through

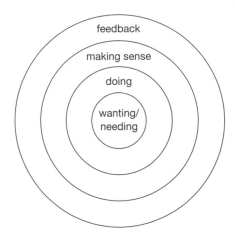

Figure 2.1 Race's ripples
Reproduced by permission of Sage Publications

experience, which makes it especially relevant to learning on placement. Race suggests that effective learning consists of 'wanting', 'doing', 'making sense' and receiving 'feedback'. This idea is explored in more detail below. The quotes from students show what these different aspects of learning might mean in the context of a social work placement.

- **Wanting/needing**
  Although we can sometimes learn without wanting to, the best learning comes from being motivated to acquire new knowledge.

  > Motivation is important on placement; if you lose it, it can be hard to keep going. I had to keep telling myself that it was all about becoming a qualified social worker and I needed to grab every opportunity.
  >
  > SAMERA *second-year student*

- **Doing**
  Your placement is all about learning from experience. You will almost certainly have opportunities to do things you haven't done before. It is important to see these as valuable learning experiences and to be prepared to have a go at new things.

  > I helped to run a group for foster parents on my second-year placement. I was really nervous at the beginning and the first couple of sessions didn't go that well, but my co-facilitator gave me lots of support and some honest feedback and it got much better. I learnt loads.
  >
  > ELLEN *second-year student*

- **Making sense**
  Even if you practise a skill or an activity over and over again, you probably won't learn much unless you take time to think about and digest or make sense of what went well and what can be improved upon next time.

  > 66 You have to give yourself time to think – you're there to learn after all.
  >
  > YASMIN *second-year student*

- **Feedback**
  Race suggests that there are two kinds of feedback. *Intrinsic* is the feedback that you give yourself when you reflect on your experiences and *extrinsic* is the feedback that you get from other people.

  > 66 It can be difficult to ask for feedback and it can be painful, but it's a very good way to learn.
  >
  > JODIE *second-year student*

Interestingly, Race has recently added two more 'ripples' to his diagram to represent *teaching* and *assessing* (see www.phil-race.co.uk). These are particularly useful and relevant additions in relation to social work placements, where the role of your practice educator as both a teacher and an assessor is crucial to the process of your learning for practice.

Kolb's learning cycle

David Kolb (1984) suggests that adult learning can be described as a four-stage cycle (see Figure 2.2). Kolb's stages have a lot in common with Honey and Mumford's learning styles and Race's ripples, but here they are seen as an ongoing circle of learning. According to this model any 'concrete' experience you have as a learner is followed by a period of sense making or 'reflective observation' on your experience. Reflection then moves into what Kolb calls 'abstract conceptualisation'. In other words, you draw out the learning or conclusions from your reflection in order to apply them to a similar situation in the future. Kolb's term for this application of your ideas to a new situation is 'active experimentation'. The new situation to which you apply your learning is a new 'concrete experience' and so the cycle begins again. Within Kolb's model the ongoing and continuous nature of the cycle of learning is particularly important.

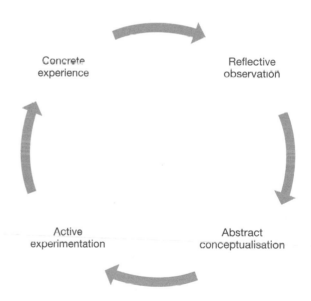

Figure 2.2 Kolb's four-stage cycle
Adapted with the permission of Pearson Education Inc.

Getting to grips with reflection

What is reflection?

Reflection is a concept that has been written about a lot in social work literature and is seen as particularly important in relation to learning on placement. The term 'reflection' is used in slightly different ways by different writers according to the particular model they are presenting. In most cases, though, Kolb's model described above or similar circular frameworks are used to depict reflection as a cycle within which practitioners learn by making sense of practice experiences and applying their learning to new experiences. Donald Schön (1983) has been particularly influential in relating reflection to *professional* knowledge and action and his ideas have been widely applied to social work. Jan Fook (2002; Fook and Gardner 2007) and others have built on Schön's work to develop more *critical* models of reflection which explicitly seek to question the status quo and promote an awareness of issues of power and powerlessness.

Models of reflection

Gibbs's model

Graham Gibbs offers a model of reflection which expands Kolb's learning cycle and helpfully adapts it to professional practice (Gibbs 1988). This model uses language that is more accessible than Kolb's (see Figure 2.3). It also incorporates reflection on feeling and guides you more explicitly through the detailed stages of reflection on practice.

Jan Fook's (1996) 'Identify, Reflect and Develop' model, adapted here (Figure 2.4), from a version

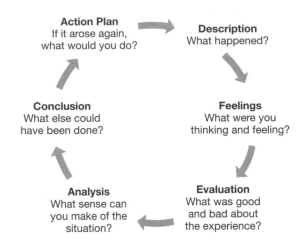

Figure 2.3 Gibbs's model of reflection

by Audrey Beverley and Aiden Worsley (2007), is helpful in encouraging you to dig below the surface and ask yourself some difficult questions. Unlike many other writers, Fook does not use a circular model, but she does encourage you to ask in detail what learning you will carry forward from each experience of reflecting on practice. By doing this, your learning from the reflective process moves you to the next episode of reflection on the next piece of practice, in a similar way to Gibbs's cyclical model.

Critical reflection

The 'identify, reflect and develop' model is more explicitly *critical* than the preceding models. It prompts you to question taken-for-granted assumptions and view situations from different perspectives. Importantly, it also requires you, the practitioner, to look at your own values and beliefs and the way these are inevitably embedded in

Identify and describe the practice experience and its context
Be as concrete and specific as possible. Context should include issues which are important, e.g., organisational issues, professional issues, time of day or week, other people involved.

Reflect on the account
What themes emerge? How are thoughts, feelings and interpretations connected? What interpretations did I make and whose interpretations are they? How did my interpretations influence the situation? How might the situation have been interpreted differently by someone else from a different perspective? What assumptions are implied from my account? Where do these assumptions come from? Are they mine? Where are the gaps and biases in my account?

Develop
How does what happened compare with what I thought would happen? Was the theory I thought I was acting upon different from what is implied by my actions? What is similar or different about this experience compared with other experiences I have had? How does my practice need to be changed as a result of this experience?

Figure 2.4 Fook's 'identify, reflect and develop' model

your individual practice. This self-awareness of the impact you will have on the situation in which you are working is called *reflexivity* and is an important component of critical reflection.

Critical reflection is also characterised by an awareness of the use of power in social situations (Howe 2009). The language people use to define themselves and others is seen as particularly significant in reflecting and helping to entrench existing unequal power relations. This critical awareness of the way power is used and misused links critical approaches closely with those social work values which are to do with promoting empowerment and social justice. For Jan Fook (2002, 2007) and others, a critically reflective approach to practice involves social workers in working alongside service users to challenge inequality and oppression.

As your placement progresses, you can ensure that your reflection becomes more critical by developing an awareness of the impact of your own values, beliefs and assumptions on the situations in which you are working. One way of approaching this is to think about the way you talk about and to service users and the language you hear others using. One obvious example is the way workers often have their own professional 'jargon', which effectively prevents service users and sometimes other workers from having access to particular knowledge and information. You can find out more about critical reflection by following up the 'further reading' at the end of this chapter.

Tools for learning

Reflective diaries

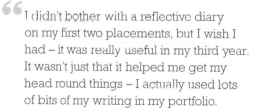

> " I didn't bother with a reflective diary on my first two placements, but I wish I had – it was really useful in my third year. It wasn't just that it helped me get my head round things – I actually used lots of bits of my writing in my portfolio.
>
> **DOMINIC** *final-year student*

Diaries come in all shapes and forms, from a simple record of appointments to a highly personal account of your innermost thoughts and feelings. A 'reflective diary' can also be shaped in whatever ways are helpful to you, but, most importantly, it is a tool for the development of your learning on placement.

The reflective diary is a writing space where you can go through the reflective process of making sense of your placement experiences and using them to build your own theories for practice. You can of course share your diary with others and you might use it to provide evidence for assessment, like the student quoted above, but many people simply find it helpful to have a private place in which to make sense of their thoughts.

> 66 I couldn't believe how far I'd come when I looked back at what I'd written at the beginning of the placement. There was so much I didn't understand and so much I was scared of. It did help me see how much I'd learnt. Mind you, it also helped me realise how much more I'd need to learn once I got into practice.
>
> DOMINIC *final-year student*

You may argue that you have a private place for reflection – inside your head – and you don't need to write your thoughts down. While this is certainly true, the great advantage of a diary is that it gives you a record of your thoughts, feelings and ideas. You will have many new experiences during your placement and it can be very helpful to see how your ideas and skills have progressed.

The diary is a good place for thinking about how to apply theory to practice. You can use it to note down ideas or quotes from your reading that have particular relevance to your practice on placement and link these to experiences as you go along. Moving through the reflective process in your diary may also help you to identify gaps in your knowledge and understanding. You might find that you need to go away and research some areas of knowledge before you can complete the theory-making stage which Kolb (1984) calls 'abstract conceptualisation', Gibbs (1988) refers to as 'action planning' and Fook (1996) as 'development'.

You might feel that you have got enough 'work' to do while you are on placement and that writing a reflective diary is too time consuming. This is completely understandable, but it is also important to remember that the diary is something that is just for you. Unlike most of the other things you'll be doing, it won't be seen or judged by anyone else; its purpose is simply to help you to cope with the placement experience and to make the rest of the 'work' easier. Here are some tips which might help you to keep going and enjoy writing your reflective diary:

> **Remember ...**
> your diary is not just for reflecting on things that go wrong – you can learn a lot from reflecting on things that go well too.

- ☑ The diary is a personal document; there is no right and wrong way of writing it.
- ☑ Don't worry about grammar and spelling.

- ☑ Include poems, drawings and ramblings if you want to.
- ☑ Have a positive approach – treat the diary as a friend not as an enemy.
- ☑ Be honest. You will only be fooling yourself if you're not.
- ☑ Focus on issues that are important to you.
- ☑ Leave spaces between your diary entries so that you can go back and reflect on these at a later stage.
- ☑ Don't feel that you have to come to conclusions. Generating more questions is an important part of the 'theory making' and 'active experimentation' parts of the reflective cycle.

Knowledge maps

Some people find that bringing ideas together in a visual way is helpful to their learning. 'Knowledge maps' or 'mind maps' are popular study skills techniques, which, several commentators claim, reflect the way in which the human brain works more accurately than conventional note taking. As well as being a useful way of making notes, knowledge maps can help you to make sense of the different areas of knowledge that might help you to understand particular practice situations. Beverley and Worsley (2007) suggest that this technique is particularly useful if you place the service user or client at the centre of your diagram as in Figure 2.5. You could, however, use the same method in relation to a supervision session, team meeting or any other placement experience.

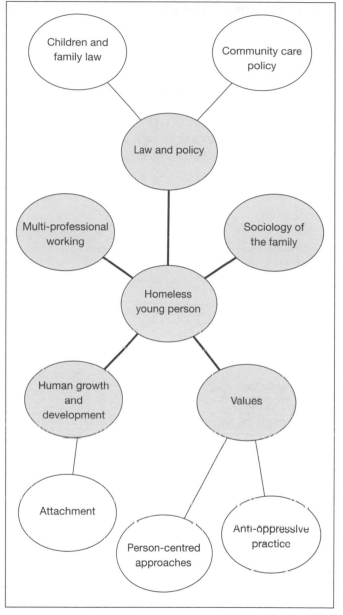

Figure 2.5 Knowledge map

Critical Incident Analysis

The Critical Incident Analysis is a way of exploring, in detail, any specific event that happens to you during your placement. It could be something quite large, like an interview that didn't go well, or something smaller like a difficult telephone call or a tense moment with a colleague. A simple version of the Critical Incident Analysis technique (Beverley and Worsley 2007) is illustrated in Figure 2.6. This model asks you to recall your feelings at

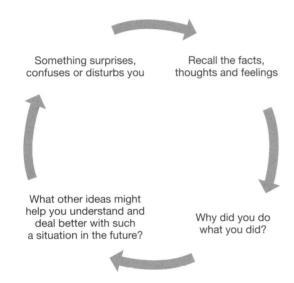

Something surprises, confuses or disturbs you

Recall the facts, thoughts and feelings

Why did you do what you did?

What other ideas might help you understand and deal better with such a situation in the future?

Figure 2.6 Critical Incident Analysis
Reproduced with the permission of Palgrave Macmillan

the time of the incident and unpick your reasons for responding in the way you did. Like several of the models discussed earlier, it takes a circular format. This underlines the importance of reflective approaches to learning for practice and the way in

which these lead you to use your learning from one incident in relation to future events. You can find out more about Critical Incident Analysis and the other tools for learning by following up the 'further reading' at the end of the chapter.

Finally ...

Learning in and for practice is difficult and personally challenging, but this chapter has shown that there are many things you can do to help make your placement a good learning experience:

- Identify and build on your existing knowledge and experience.
- Be honest about the things you need to learn and give yourself permission not to know things.
- Take control of your learning.
- Be prepared to reflect honestly and critically on your practice.

Further reading and resources

A. Beverley and A. Worsley, *Learning and Teaching in Social Work Practice* (Basingstoke: Palgrave Macmillan, 2007). This book has some good material on creating and using learning opportunities and is particularly useful for adult learners.

J. Lishman (ed.), *Handbook for Practice Learning in Social Work and Social Care: Knowledge and Theory*, 2nd edition (London: Jessica Kingsley, 2007). Jan Fook's chapter, 'Reflective Practice and Critical Reflection', will help you understand this concept further.

www.phil-race.co.uk/ is Phil Race's own website with information about adult learning and making the most of your learning.

www.peterhoney.com/ is the site of Peter Honey (of Honey and Mumford discussed in this chapter). You can download the most recent version of his Learning Styles Questionnaire here (for a fee).

http://www.studygs.net/mapping/ shows you how to use knowledge maps.

3 Using theory and knowledge in practice

This chapter will help you to ...

- **Recognise the ways we all use theory all the time in everyday life**
- **Understand why theory is important for social work practice**
- **Use formal and informal theoretical knowledge in practice**
- **Understand the different kinds of knowledge used in social work**
- **Link knowledge, skills and values in your practice**

66 It's a good feeling when you use something you've read to explain what's happening in a practice situation. It makes you feel like you've really got something to contribute.

YASMIN *second-year student*

66 There was a bit of me thought that social work was just common sense or that the stuff we'd learnt in college wasn't really relevant to placement, but you realise after a while that you need it to make sense of what you're doing.

SAMERA *second-year student*

As a social worker you will draw on a wide range of knowledge to help you understand different situations and guide your practice. This will include theories about why things are the way they are, findings from research and all sorts of other published writing about the knowledge, skills and values that underpin social work. You will also learn a great deal during your placement from watching and listening to more experienced social workers and by reflecting on your own experiences. Together, these different forms of knowledge or *evidence* represent an invaluable guide to *how*, *when* and *why* to intervene in practice situations.

The first part of the chapter focuses on understanding theories and theoretical knowledge and then moves on to look more widely at the way the different sorts of knowledge referred to above fit together to inform practice. Even if, like Samera, the student quoted, you sometimes find it hard to see the relevance of underpinning knowledge to your work on placement, this chapter will help you to find ways you are comfortable with, of talking and writing about theoretical and other knowledge in relation to your own practice. The list of reading and resources at the end of the chapter gives you some suggestions about finding research evidence

and useful reading about theory for practice. In addition to this you will have your own sources of knowledge gathered from your university course, and the support of your practice educator in identifying and applying knowledge which is particularly relevant to your placement.

Theory in everyday life

Theory often gets associated with highly academic or scientific knowledge and the most difficult aspects of learning and understanding. For this reason it can seem like a specialised activity which doesn't have much to do with everyday life. In fact, theorising is much more of an everyday activity than you might think. We construct theories all the time about why things happen and how people behave from day to day. Some writers even argue that it is psychologically impossible *not* to have theories about things (Sheldon 1995; Trevithick 2005).

It is important to understand that theory goes beyond description to *explain why* things happen in a particular way and so to *predict* how and why they may happen in the future. Exercise 3.1 shows how we instinctively do this all the time.

Think about a time when someone has behaved towards you in a way that you found difficult to understand and see if you can think of a possible explanation. We have provided an example to start you off. Your example could be as simple as a person being rude to you at work or someone being unexpectedly excited when you meet them.

Behaviour	Possible explanations
Example: Woman in supermarket shouting very loudly at her child	☑ She might be very stressed by things happening in her life (relationship problems, lack of money) and is taking this out on the child ☑ Child may have behavioural problems that she is finding it difficult to deal with ☑ She may be suffering from postnatal depression or some other mental health issue ☑ She may be behaving in the way her own mother behaved towards her
Your example:	

The possible explanations you have listed are ideas about why things happen in the way that they do. In other words, they are ways of making sense of a situation. These initial ideas or *hypotheses* need to be tested through research or further investigation before they become a fully developed theory. Nevertheless, you can see that you have already created some possible explanations which might be used to predict future behaviour in similar situations.

As a social worker in our example above you would of course get to know the woman and her child much better. Alongside this, you would probably use theoretical knowledge from your reading and college learning to develop a detailed theory to explain much more fully what is happening in this situation. The next section looks at how you might go about this and why theory is particularly important for social work practice.

The importance of theory for social work practice

What is theory for social work?

Chris Beckett (2006: 24) describes theory as: 'Ideas and models which we can use to make sense of the situations we find ourselves in and/or help us to shape our responses.'

The previous exercise showed how we instinctively develop theories in our daily lives. As a social work student on placement, however, you will be expected to go beyond the sort of day-to-day theorising we all do instinctively to provide more detailed explanations and reasons for choosing to work in particular ways with different service users. Fortunately, many ideas and models have emerged from years of social work writing and research, which you can use to ensure that your work with service users is as good as it can be. As Chris Beckett points out, these ideas and models are what we mean by theory for social work.

> **Remember ...** using theory is all about making sense of a situation and helping you decide what should happen next.

Coping with contradictions between theories

As you become more experienced at reading about and applying theory for social work, you will become increasingly aware of contradictions between one theory and another. For example, there are several different theories of bereavement.

While these overlap in several respects, they also highlight disagreements between different writers or 'schools' of thought about the usefulness of particular theoretical models. These disagreements and alternative models can seem confusing. However, understanding that they exist will help you to make sense of your reading and begin to decide which theoretical models and perspectives you favour.

Developing a *narrative* of theoretical knowledge

The idea of favouring one set of theories over another may feel like quite a challenge, particularly if you are at an early stage in your training. However, the more you learn, the more you will find that some ideas make greater sense to you and seem more relevant to your practice than others. It is important to give yourself permission to prefer certain perspectives or to favour the work of one writer over another. You will probably also find that you use *elements* of different theories in order to understand and intervene in practice. Drawing on elements of different theories will enable you to develop your own particular *narrative* of theoretical knowledge to explain what is going on in any given situation. The term 'narrative' is used several times in the remainder of this chapter to talk about the way different theories or elements of different theories can helpfully be brought together.

Using theory in practice

As we've seen above, theory provides ways of enabling you to make sense of a situation in order to ensure that you respond or intervene in the most helpful and appropriate way possible. The next exercise asks you to think about the range of theoretical knowledge that might be useful in a particular situation. As you gain practice experience on placement, you will be able to make further links between theoretical knowledge and real practice situations.

Exercise 3.2 relates to a particular practice situation; you can easily substitute this with an example from your placement.

Some of the possible explanations and associated theories or areas of theoretical knowledge you may have identified include:

- Jane may be responding to the long-term pressure of caring. This could be having an impact on her own mental health. (*Theories of carer stress; specific theories of depression and mental illness*)
- Jane may have undergone a number of losses including her job and other roles. She may also feel that in some ways she has lost the mother she once had. Elsa may feel that she has lost her independence and *her* role as a mother. (*Theories of bereavement and loss*)
- There may be long-term difficulties in the relationship between Elsa and Jane, which may or may not be openly acknowledged. These could be to do with issues from Jane's childhood. (*Attachment theory; theories of adult relationships and the life course*)

3

Exercise 3.2 **Working with theoretical knowledge**

Look at the case example below and list some possible explanations for the deterioration in Jane and Elsa's relationship. Try to move beyond the sort of day-to-day theorising you did in the first exercise. This time, see if you can draw on the areas of theoretical knowledge you have read and learnt about during your training so far. This should help you to make sense of what is happening and so decide how best to help Jane and Elsa.

Jane is a full-time carer for her mother Elsa who has dementia. The professionals working with Jane and Elsa say that the relationship between the two women seems to have deteriorated badly in recent weeks and additional help is needed if Jane is to continue in her role.

Possible explanations and associated theories

- _____
- _____
- _____
- _____

- Jane may feel that as a woman she has been pressured into taking on the caring role. She may feel ambivalent or angry about this. (*Theories of gender*)

These are just some of the areas of theoretical knowledge you may find helpful in explaining Jane and Elsa's situation. We could have included several others. At the moment the ideas on the list and their associated theories are still *hypotheses* which would need to be tested out through your conversations with the two women, with others involved and through further reading and reflection. This ongoing work will enable you to refine and develop your hypothesis in order to develop your own narrative of the theoretical knowledge you are using to explain this situation, until you feel that you have the most accurate understanding possible in order to decide how best to help Jane and Elsa.

You can see from this example that using theory often involves trying out ideas and being prepared to change or refine them as your knowledge and understanding of the situation changes.

Formal and informal theoretical knowledge

There are several ways of thinking and talking about the different kinds of theoretical knowledge used by social workers. One helpful division is into *formal* and *informal* theoretical knowledge.

Formal theoretical knowledge

Formal theoretical knowledge includes the sorts of theories which seek to *explain* why things happen in particular ways. Most of the discussion in this chapter so far has been about theories which explain. Theories which offer ways in which you might *intervene* to help people as a social worker also come into the category of formal theoretical knowledge.

Theories that explain

The theories used by social workers to explain and make sense of situations tend to come from a range of disciplines. Pamela Trevithick (2005) identifies sociology, psychology, social policy, philosophy, economics, organisational studies, law and medicine as areas of study from which social work has borrowed theory. Most of these areas (with the exception of medicine) can be broadly classified as social science rather than natural science. The theories they use therefore tend not to be scientifically testable in the way that a theory from natural science might be. This is one reason why, as we have already seen, the theories used in social work can be contradictory and subject to disagreement.

Social work
- Sociology
- Psychology
- Social policy
- Philosophy
- Economics
- Organisational studies
- Law
- Medicine

Theories that explain or 'explanatory theories' are used in a number of different ways in relation to social work:

- Some theories are used by social workers to explain how society is organised or structured. These are usually large-scale, overarching theories such as feminism, postmodernism or the many theories dealing with power relations. They tend to be applicable in almost any circumstance and can be used in conjunction with other, more situation-specific theories to develop a narrative of theoretical knowledge.

- Some theories are used to explain individual experiences or situations. Examples include theories of attachment or bereavement and loss, where the explanation being sought relates to one person or one family/group of people. Again, these sorts of theories may be used in conjunction with others in order to create a narrative of theoretical knowledge.
- Many explanatory theories contain elements of *both* the individual and the structural. Good examples of this are labelling theory and theories

of social exclusion, which have something to say about the way in which society operates (to label or exclude groups of people) *and* seek to explain individual experience.

- Some theories seek to *explain* social work itself. You will come across theories about the state of social work and how social work ought to be. For example, some theories suggest that social work today is entirely to do with calculating risk; others argue that it should be all about social justice. These explanatory theories will help you develop your own informed views about social work and about what sort of practitioner you want to become. Now try Exercise 3.3.

Exercise 3.3 Explanatory theories

Use the table below to begin to make notes about the kinds of explanation offered by different explanatory theories. Try to choose theories you think you have used or might be able to use during your placement.

Explanatory theory	What does the theory tell you about:		
	Society	*Individual experience*	*Social work*
• Labelling theory	Society has a need to identify groups of people by using labels	Prompts you to think about how would it feel to be labelled	The importance for social workers of empathising with individuals and avoiding labelling service users
•			
•			

One of the things you will realise from doing the exercise above is that explanatory theories do not tell you how to *do* social work. Rather they provide helpful insights on which you can draw in your practice. These insights will help you develop an explanation of the situations you are working in and why you make particular practice choices in relation to each service user.

Theories that help you intervene

Theories that help you to intervene, or 'intervention theories', are about particular ways of *doing* social work. These are sometimes called 'methods' or 'practice approaches'. It doesn't really matter which of these words or phrases you use as long as you feel comfortable with your choice.

> **Doing social work**
> • Intervention theories
> • Practice approaches
> • Methods

Intervention theories are used in a number of different ways in relation to social work:

• Some intervention theories offer very explicit practice guidance. Examples include 'task-centred', 'solution-focused' and 'crisis intervention' approaches. It is possible that your work with a particular service user may be dominated by one approach, either because it is favoured by your agency or because you judge that it will be particularly effective in this situation. It is more likely, however, that you will draw on *elements* of different practice approaches according to the context and the individuals involved. As with explanatory theories (above) it is important that you are able to use these to develop an explanation or *narrative* about why

and how you are doing social work in a particular way in any given situation.

• Some intervention theories are more general and tend to offer broad principles for intervention rather than explicit guidance. Examples are 'person-centred' approaches and 'anti-oppressive practice'. Theories like this give you important underpinning principles for how to go about social work, without necessarily providing explicit techniques. They are often closely linked to the value base of social work. Again, these theories are an important part of your narrative of how and why you are making particular practice choices.

• Some intervention theories are underpinned by broader explanatory theories. Crisis Intervention, for example, offers an explicit practice approach, which is underpinned by an explanation of human responses drawn from psychodynamic theory.

You should begin to see from Exercise 3.4 that intervention theories are not mutually exclusive, but are often combined with each other and with different explanatory theories. They are also often combined with *informal* theoretical knowledge; you can read more about this below.

Informal theoretical knowledge

Informal theoretical knowledge is drawn from a range of sources and is used in a number of different ways in relation to social work. It includes the sort of understanding you develop through the process of reflecting on your *personal experience* and *practice wisdom* as well as the knowledge and

Use the table below to make notes about intervention theories you have used or plan to use in relation to particular practice activities. In the right-hand column, begin to make notes about *how* you have drawn on these theories.

Practice activity	Intervention theory	Narrative of *how* the intervention theory was used
E.g. initial meeting with service user 'A'	E.g. Task-centred theory E.g. Person-centred theory	Worked in partnership with A to draw up list of agreed goals. Agreed tasks A will complete by next time we meet. Sought to use empathy and unconditional positive regard to understand and avoid easy judgements of things I found difficult. Used listening and communication skills to get as full a picture of A's situation as possible.

3

understanding you gain from service users and carers about their life experiences and individual situations. Informal theoretical knowledge tends to be more fluid and less fixed than formal theoretical knowledge and is likely to be used in different ways at different times.

Remember ... social workers are entitled to develop their own theory for practice, but this needs to be coherent and supported by strong evidence.

Personal and practice experience

Your past personal experiences can be useful in helping you to theorise by developing a *hypothesis* about a practice situation. It is important to recognise that your life experiences cannot necessarily be universalised and that other people's experiences of similar situations may be very different. Nevertheless personal experience can offer important insights for practice.

Similarly, you will find that the experience you build up on placement and later as a qualified social worker will help to inform your future practice. This *practice wisdom* will become increasingly important in helping you to decide why and how to intervene in social work situations.

As a professional, your rationalisation for intervention in any situation needs to be fully developed and coherent. This means that you will probably need to draw on additional evidence such as formal theories or research findings in order to support your knowledge from personal or practice experience.

Service user and carer expertise

You will learn a great deal during your placement and throughout your future career from the people who are receiving a service from your organisation. The term 'experts by experience' is increasingly used by both service user-led organisations and by professionals seeking greater involvement from service users and carers. It is a term that recognises the wealth of knowledge held by service users about a diverse range of life experiences and about what it is really like to be on the receiving end of social work practice.

Fitting it all together: theoretical knowledge for practice

Table 3.1 lists a few examples of the different kinds of formal and informal theoretical knowledge we have been discussing. You will be able to think of many more examples as your learning progresses.

Another way of thinking about the sort of theoretical knowledge we have looked at so far is in terms of a jigsaw puzzle that has pieces which fit together to make a coherent whole (Figure 3.1).

Figure 3.1 Theoretical knowledge for practice

Table 3.1 Formal and informal knowledge

Formal theoretical knowledge		Informal theoretical knowledge		
Theories that explain	Theories to help you intervene	Personal experience	Practice experience	Service user expertise
E.g. • Attachment • Feminism • Power • Theories about the social work role	E.g. • Task-centred • Solution-focused • Crisis intervention	E.g. • Experience of bereavement • Experience of caring for an elderly relative	E.g. • Ways of breaking bad news • Techniques for ending conversations sensitively	E.g. • Experience of living in poverty • Experience of mental health services

Other kinds of knowledge for social work

Theory or 'theoretical knowledge' is just one of several kinds of professional knowledge you will need in order to be an effective social worker. An important skill for all social workers is the ability to bring these different kinds of knowledge together. Useful areas of knowledge for social work include procedural knowledge, legal and policy knowledge, empirical knowledge, and knowledge about services and resources

Procedural knowledge

Procedural knowledge has become increasingly important in social work in recent years. It refers to the ways in which your organisation requires you work. This could be to do with things that are specific to your agency such as procedures for signing in and out of the office or rules about where personal information can and cannot be stored. Alternatively, procedures may be closely linked to legislation and national policies such as recording your work in particular ways or completing written documents to specified time scales. Adhering to specific procedures will probably be an essential requirement of the organisation in which you are placed. However, it is also important to reflect critically on any rules which impact on your practice and be aware of the political and organisational agendas that may underpin them.

Legal and policy knowledge

As you will know, the law is very important in social work. If your placement is in a local authority, a health trust or another statutory agency, you will be working very specifically to enact certain laws and government policies. Even if you are placed in a private or voluntary agency, your role will be closely related to the law in your particular area of practice. This does not mean that everything you do is specified and controlled. Law and policy gives you a framework within which to work, but the approach you take to the way in which you work with individuals is subject to your own judgement and theoretical approach.

Empirical knowledge

This is knowledge which comes from systematic research. It might be research carried out and published by your agency, or published in journal articles or on government or health and social care websites. It is not always possible to separate research knowledge from theoretical knowledge because research is often used to test particular theories and theories are sometimes built from research findings.

In this chapter we have talked about 'evidence' in relation to the many different kinds of knowledge which inform or underpin practice. Sometimes, however, the term 'evidence-based practice' is used specifically to describe the way research findings can be used to establish knowledge about the social world and so identify what sort of interventions work best in particular situations. Empirical knowledge can often be used alongside theoretical knowledge in helping you to decide what kind of intervention to make and how best to go about it.

3

Knowledge about services and resources

There will be all sorts of services and resources available to the people you are working with during your placement. These will vary according to the locality in which you are working, the client group you are working with and the particular kind of service offered by your agency. There are no short cuts to this sort of knowledge and no one will blame you for not knowing everything. You may find that your agency has a resource base where you can look up some of this information. You will probably also be surprised at how much local information you pick up during the course of your placement.

Fitting different kinds of knowledge into the jigsaw

If we continue with the image of a jigsaw puzzle, you can see that the different kinds of knowledge for practice listed above can be brought together with the theoretical knowledge we discussed earlier, to create an even more detailed picture of the knowledge needed for social work practice (Figure 3.2).

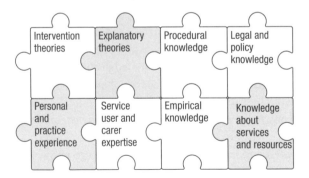

Figure 3.2 Knowledge for practice

Linking knowledge, skills and values

Skills for social work practice

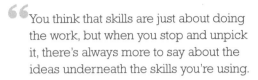

> You think that skills are just about doing the work, but when you stop and unpick it, there's always more to say about the ideas underneath the skills you're using.

WILF *third-year student*

This chapter has focused mainly on the use of theoretical knowledge, but in order to complete the jigsaw of knowledge for effective social work practice, we need to add *skills* and *values* to the picture. If theory is about the ideas and models we use to make sense of situations and shape our responses, then skills are the tools we use to put these responses into practice. This means that theory and skills for social work are closely entwined, as the student quoted suggests.

Some of the detailed skills listed in Exercise 3.5, particularly the final three, come from 'person-centred' counselling. While this is not explicitly a social work approach, the techniques within it have been influential  in social work practice. Person-centred counselling could be described as an 'intervention theory' in that it offers a range of specific techniques for talking, listening and being with people. So the

Exercise 3.5 | Social work skills

Begin by making a list of all the skills you think you might need during your placement.

_____

_____

_____

_____

_____

_____

_____

_____

_____

_____

You will probably find that you can quite quickly create a very long list indeed. In her book on social work skills, Pamela Trevithick (2005: 82) lists 50 different 'skills and interventions' that social workers commonly use in their practice. Your list may not be as long as Trevithick's, but you can probably extend it by breaking down some of the skills you have identified. For example, 'communication skills', noted above, could include:

- Open questions
- Closed questions
- Paraphrasing
- Clarifying
- Summarising
- 'What' questions
- Prompting
- Probing
- Allowing and using silences
- Using self-disclosure
- Empathy
- Congruence
- Unconditional positive regard

skills listed are some of the tools you need to put one particular intervention theory into practice. If you were to dig even deeper, you could say that the person-centred counselling has its roots in humanism, a theory which _explains_ human motivation in terms of fulfilment and growth. In other words, humanism is the _explanatory theory_ behind person-centred counselling, which is the _intervention theory_ needing some of the _skills_ on our list in order for it to be put into practice.

Of course, not every skill can be or needs to be unpicked in quite such depth. However, it is always worth asking where the idea comes from that a particular skill is useful in practice. This is an example of critical thinking which will not only help you to understand why you are doing what you are doing, but will also help you to decide which skills to use in any particular situation.

Values for social work practice

The final and very important piece in our jigsaw of knowledge for practice is _values_. This is because your values as a person and as a practitioner need to underpin everything you do in social work.

As a social worker in England you will be expected to practise in accordance with the Code of Practice for Social Care Workers (General Social Care Council 2002) and the National Occupational Standards for Social Work (Topss/Skills for Care 2002; see Appendix A in this book). The Care Councils for each of the other regions and nations in the UK have their own, similar codes of practice and occupational standards (see Appendix B in this book, which covers standards in Scotland). You may also draw on other national and international codes of values and ethics for social work (e.g., British Association of Social Workers 2002; International Federation of Social Workers/International Association of Schools of Social Work 2004).

The values that inform your practice will probably be a combination of these formal professional codes and the beliefs that make you the unique individual you are. On their own these values will be of limited use. Beliefs and good intentions will not give you the knowledge or the skills you need to make sense of a practice situation and intervene in it. However, without values you will not be able to make *choices* about *how* to use knowledge and skills in any specific practice situation.

Go back to Exercise 3.2 and the story of Jane and Elsa. In this situation you may identify one or more explanatory theories to understand what is going on and you may consider a number of possible interventions. In the end, however, your choice of *how* to intervene will depend on your beliefs about the rights that Jane and Elsa have to make choices and experience similar freedoms to others. These are questions of values, rather than theory, knowledge or skills. The list of further reading at the end of this chapter includes two books on values in social work, which both contain lots of exercises and activities to help you think about values in relation to your own practice.

Our final version of the jigsaw puzzle, with the addition of skills and values, looks complicated (Figure 3.3). As we have seen in this chapter, however, each piece signifies something that can be clearly understood in relation to practice. Not

only that, the various pieces fit together to make a unified whole, representing the totality of the knowledge you need to be an effective social worker.

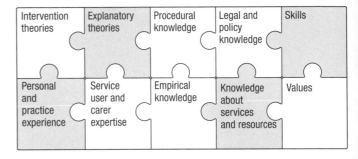

Figure 3.3 Knowledge, skills and values for practice

Finally ...

Theory can be difficult to get to grips with and sometimes seems hard to apply to social work practice, but this chapter has shown how closely theory relates to other kinds of knowledge for practice. Remember:

- Theory is not something mysterious; it's something we all use all the time.
- Using theory will help you to be a better social worker.
- Theory is just one piece in the jigsaw of knowledge, skills and values needed for social work practice.

Further reading and resources

A. Barnard, N. Horner and J. Wild (eds), *The Value Base of Social Work and Social Care: An Active Learning Handbook* (Maidenhead: McGraw-Hill/ Open University Press, 2008). This provides practical and straightforward accounts of values and ethics in social work.

D. Howe, *A Brief Introduction to Social Work Theory* (Basingstoke: Palgrave Macmillan, 2009). This is a clear, accessible book, which will help you develop your understanding of social work theory.

www.rip.org.uk is the website of Research in Practice which supports evidenced-informed practice with children and families.

www.ripfa.org.uk is the website of Research in Practice for Adults, for evidenced-informed adult social work practice.

www.scie.org.uk is the Social Care Institute for Excellence website, which provides evidenced-informed research for practice generically.

www.uca.ac.uk/menu/acad_depts/swk/MRC_web/ public_html/ is the website of Making Research Count, a network of ten university departments of social work, committed to making social work research more widely available.

3

4 Keeping service users central to your learning and practice

This chapter will help you to ...

- Understand the context of service user and carer involvement and participation in social work
- Draw on a number of models of service user participation during your placement
- Plan ways of seeking service user and carer feedback on your practice and using it creatively
- Understand the link between social work values and service user participation

"I remember my practice assessor was really into me getting feedback from the young people I was working with – she got me to set up a system for doing it in induction and encouraged me to read about service users. It really helped me focus on them.

SARA *newly qualified social worker*

"You know it was only when I got out on my second year placement that the light bulb suddenly went on! I realised that this job is about the people we work with. I was so absorbed with college life, I had forgotten the main reason for doing the job.

EVE *third-year student*

During a busy placement it is easy to forget about the real reason you are there. Whatever terminology you use – 'service users', 'clients', 'patients' or 'customers' – the fact remains that *people* are at the heart of social work. This chapter will help you to understand why service user participation and the promotion of equality are central to the value base underpinning social work practice. It will also help you to keep service users at the centre of your practice and to learn from their experiences and expertise.

You might think that the people who use social work services are automatically 'involved' in everything that social workers do. While this is true to some extent, you will know from your learning about power and anti-oppressive practice that the potential power imbalance between social workers and service users is very great indeed. There is not enough space in this chapter to explore issues of power and oppression in detail. We will, however, provide some specific models and ideas about involvement and participation that you can use to think about – and perhaps even to challenge – imbalances of power during your placement. You will probably find it helpful to look at what follows alongside any notes and reading you have been given about social work and power.

The context of service user involvement and participation in social work

Historically, there has been a strong strand of thought within social work that has promoted the

idea of service users as proud, coping, independent and socially included, rather than stigmatised, weak, not coping and dependent (Beresford and Croft 2004). The idea of service user involvement and participation is very much associated with this tradition and has been widely explored through the literature on 'anti-oppressive' and, more recently, 'critical' practice.

Service user participation and involvement has been incorporated into a range of policy documents and legislation during the past 20 years. Moves towards greater involvement are reflected in many areas of local government and in health services through a range of patient partnership initiatives. In social work and social care practice, consultation with, and participation of, service users is required by the General Social Care Council (2002) (and the equivalent bodies in other parts of the UK), while colleges and universities that provide professional qualifying social work courses *must* involve service users in all aspects of training (DoH 2002).

All of this reflects a recognition within social work and within central and local government that practice can be improved (and service delivered in more cost-effective ways) if service users are involved in shaping the services they use.

Ideological approaches

There are several different ideological approaches to service user participation. Two useful approaches are outlined very briefly below and explored in Exercise 4.1. These both relate more to the way services are developed and provided within an agency or organisations as a whole than the way social workers practise with individuals. However, as a social work student on placement, you are part of an organisation. This means that the way you are seen by service users and the scope of the service you are able to offer will be affected by the ideological position of the organisation within which you are working.

- **The consumerist approach** aims to improve services by working with service users as 'active consumers'. That is, agencies try to improve their product in response to feedback from their 'consumers' (Boylan and Dalrymple 2009). If there is more than one service provider then service users can exercise their choice as consumers to go to the provider who best meets their needs. If a service falls short of its promise they can also complain.

- **The democratic approach** is 'rights and justice' based. It aims to ensure service users have involvement in the decision-making processes rather than just being recipients of the end product (Franklin 2002). This includes service users *setting the agenda* with regard to service provision, not just being seen as consumers responding to the service being provided.

Exercise 4.1	Understanding the approach of your agency

It may be that your placement agency or organisation includes consumerist *and* democratic elements within its approach to service user involvement. Use the table below to try to identify these different strands and think about how they might affect your approach to working with individuals and families.

Consumerist	Democratic
Example: use of a standard feedback form or complaint form	*Example:* service users as equal participants on a service planning group
•	•
•	•
•	•

4

Models of service user participation

Theoretical models can be a useful starting point in helping you to understand the issues involved in service user participation and in thinking about ways of keeping service users central to your learning and practice on placement. Three models, 'The Ladder', 'The Bridge' and 'The Hub and Spoke' are introduced below to help to deepen your understanding of service user perspectives and participation at an organisational level. These are followed by an approach to individual practice which will help you to keep those you work with at the centre of everything you do on placement. We have called this 'The Service User Question'.

It is important to remember, of course, that some of the people who receive social work interventions would rather not have any involvement with social workers at all. It is also the case that sometimes social workers have to make difficult professional judgements which limit the freedom of individuals or go against the choices they would make for themselves. The removal of people to hospital or another place of safety under mental health legislation and the taking of children into the care of the local authority are two obvious examples of this.

The ease with which the models outlined below can be applied to your particular placement setting will depend very much on the sort of work you are doing. However, many of the issues of power and powerlessness that they raise will be particularly applicable to those service users who have fewest choices and least say in the services they are receiving.

The Ladder Model

A lot of the literature on service user participation uses the idea of a 'ladder' to show different potential levels of service user participation. This can range from the tokenistic involvement of service users to the transfer of power, money and authority from professionals to effectively organised service user groups. Most of these models draw on Arnstein's (1969) 'Ladder of Citizen Participation'. The idea of the ladder is that the higher a service user can climb, the more genuine and effective their participation is.

Within this model the process of climbing up the ladder is important but it is also important to remember that not all service users will have the opportunity or even want to reach the top of any given ladder. Shier (2001) puts this well:

> Sometimes we use a ladder to climb to the top and move on, but very often we just want to get to a rung someway up to work at the correct height for the job we are doing, for example painting a window frame. This may be only half way up, but it is the right height for the job in hand, and it would be counterproductive to climb higher.

You may find it helpful to share Exercise 4.2 with your supervisor or practice assessor as a way of starting a discussion about service user involvement.

Remember ... there are limits to what you can achieve as a student on placement, but even a small contribution to promoting user and carer participation can make a difference.

Exercise 4.2 The Ladder of Participation: your agency

Think of ways in which your placement agency involves service users in its work.

- How seriously does the agency take the issue of service user participation?
- How could the agency move towards service users exercising partnership with agencies and professionals?

Try to fill in the ladder below in relation to your agency to help you answer these questions.

Control	Service users take control and have more say in the running of the organisation than professionals.
	Your agency ...
Partnership	Service users share power with professionals in delivering the service.
	Your agency ...
Consultation	Service users' voices are heard but they have no assurance of changing the way services are delivered.
	Your agency ...
Information	Information is given to service users and comments are received but what happens to these comments still remains with the organisation.
	Your agency ...
Manipulation	This is the level of non-participation, where all decisions are made by professionals.
	Your agency ...

The Ladder of Participation is particularly helpful for thinking about the way in which your placement agency involves service users. However, it can also be used to help you to reflect on your own social work practice.

Exercise 4.3 The Ladder of Participation: your practice

This time, try thinking about involvement and participation in your direct work with service users.

When have you been able to involve a service user in a decision about a service they were receiving?

What enabled their involvement in this particular decision?

On which rung of the Ladder of Participation would you place this involvement?

Why would you place it on this rung?

You can do this exercise again as you progress through your placement and see how far you have been able to develop your practice to meaningfully include service users in decisions about the services they receive. The ability to engage and involve service users will depend a great deal on the ethos or ideology within your agency and the systems that are in place to involve those who use services. If service user participation is not well established within the agency then it will be harder to work directly with service users on the higher rungs of the Ladder of Participation.

The Bridge Model

This model originates from Mary John (1996), who suggests that a bridge is a more helpful concept than a ladder. This is because it allows a flow of ideas, conversations and negotiations, back and forth across the bridge. It also highlights the idea that there is a 'gap' or a river to cross before service users and professionals can truly work together.

The Bridge Model has been used to explore children's participation in service delivery and development. The picture illustrates the river with adult professionals and children facing each other on different sides. The two sides are intended to represent the world of adult service providers and the world of children who often have very little power or influence over the services they receive. The river is the gap that can exist between these two groups. Within this model, the role of the social worker and the social work service is to empower and involve service users in order to 'bridge' the 'gap'.

Using this model involves ways of thinking which acknowledge

- that certain groups are stigmatised and do not have a voice (which can be heard across the river): they are both *invisible* and *unheard*
- that work on participation and involvement needs to be aimed at a structural rather than simply an individual level. In other words, social work sometimes needs to be aimed at changing wider society.

The problem of structural inequality, highlighted by the Bridge Model, clearly cannot be solved by one social work student during the course of a single placement. However, the model does give you a conceptual framework for thinking about the barriers to service user participation in service delivery. The model also highlights the fact that encouraging people to comment on the services they use can be complicated by their position in society. Exercise 4.4 is aimed at getting you to think about the issues raised by the Bridge Model and how they might relate to your practice.

These ideas about powerlessness and exclusion are complex even if the Bridge Model looks quite simple. Case Example 4.1 on the next page will help you to relate the ideas we have discussed to practice. It shows how a relatively small action can have a big impact on the life of someone who feels quite powerless. It also illustrates how empowering it can be to share experiences with others.

Exercise 4.4 Using the Bridge Model

Think about the lives of some of the people you are working with on placement and try to fill in the boxes below. While you might want to focus on social work services in particular, you may also want to think about other services such as health, housing and education, which impact on the lives of those you are working with.

1 How far do the people you are thinking about have a 'voice' or a 'say' in the things that happen to them?

2 What stops people from having a voice (e.g., fear, powerlessness, illness or disability)?

3 Are there any groups or systems which might help to give them more of a say (e.g., service user groups, patient councils, public consultations, self-help groups, advocacy service)?

4 What else might be done to bridge the gap between service users and those who provide services (e.g., groups that might be set up, feedback systems, changes to the way the service is provided)?

5 What contribution can you make as a practitioner to try to ensure that there is movement to and fro across the bridge in your individual work with service users and carers?

Katie is 10; she is a carer for her mum and dad, who both have histories of mental illness; she does not always get to school. Katie has one good friend but she is quite lonely as she cannot go to after-school activities or go out to meet friends. Katie agrees that her social worker can refer her to a Young Carer's Group. When she begins to attend Katie is amazed to find there are other children like her – there is even one who lives two roads away! Katie feels safe to talk about her life in the group and she begins to feel better. She wants to make sure other children who are carers know about the group so she takes part in a programme on young carers on local radio. Katie begins to talk more in school and to friends about her life; she does not feel ashamed any more and she knows she is not alone. This makes it okay for her to speak out. Katie is now beginning to have a voice and to 'shout across the river'.

The Hub and Spoke Model

In this model, service user participation is structured around a central hub of activity. This usually involves a group of service users meeting together with professionals involved in providing a particular service. The amount of power that service users have within the hub group will depend on which rung of the Ladder of Participation the group is positioned. Where the hub group is working well, it should be a source of mutual support for its members as well as a way of bringing together the activities of the whole group.

The spokes radiating from the hub represent specific areas of involvement which some or all of the group members are involved in. These various activities might require differing degrees of

participation and involve different group members at different times (Taylor and Dalrymple 2005).

One example of a 'hub' in adult social care is a group made up of service users and staff in a centre for carers. The hub meets once a month to co-ordinate and receive feedback on a range of activities. These are represented by the 'spokes' in the diagram. In this case the activities include involvement in staff training, the planning of a new service and facilitation of a self-help group. Some people are involved in just one of the 'spoke' activities, others take part in several, depending on their enthusiasm, expertise and the time they have available. This is illustrated in Figure 4.1.

Figure 4.1 The Hub and Spoke Model

Try completing the following table:

Activity: Inputting data about a service user on the computer	Where is the service user in this activity?
Activity: Discussion about the duty rota in team meeting	What about the service user?
Activity: Supervision session about practice learning	How does this relate to service users?

The Service User Question

The aim of 'the Service User Question' is to help you relate *all* your work on placement to the users of the service your agency provides. This is particularly useful in relation to the tasks commonly undertaken by social workers, which do not appear to immediately relate to service users.

The Service User Question can be expressed in a number of ways, but it is always aimed at reminding you to relate everything you do to the service users you are working with. So the question might be:

"Where is the service user in this activity?" *or*

"How does this relate to service users?" *or simply*

"What about the service user?"

Try completing Exercise 4.5.

Some ideas you might have included are:

1 *Computer data inputting.* A high standard of agency record keeping should help service users by ensuring that they do not have to keep repeating the same factual information about themselves to health and social care professionals. It should also promote accountability and the effective allocation of resources. If these systems are working well, they can play an important part in ensuring that current and future service users receive the fairest and best possible service.

2 *Duty rota discussion.* Well-organised, well-managed teams, with an effective duty system, have a real and significant impact on the quality of the service provided. For many people, their first contact with an agency or organisation is through the duty system. If this is working well, the chances of establishing a good relationship with the service user from the beginning are greatly increased.

3 *Supervision.* Safe and effective social work practice is underpinned by regular professional supervision (Chapter 5, *Making the most of supervision*, takes you through the process of making the most of supervision in detail). This is important for you and also for those you are working with. Good supervision will help you to develop confidence and professionalism. This, in turn, will have a direct impact on the quality of your work with service users.

Using the table below, see if you can identify some activities from your own placement which do not immediately seem relevant to the service users you are working with. How can you relate the activity to the service users' needs and welfare?

Keeping the Service User Question in mind will help you to integrate the different agendas, perspectives and demands on your time that characterise most social work placements.

The models we have looked at all aim to help you understand the complex nature of service user participation and why it is important to keep the service user central to you practice and to your learning.

Exercise 4.5 cont'd	The Service User Question
Activity:	How does this relate to service users?
Activity:	Where is the service user in this activity?
Activity:	What about the service user?

As a student on placement one of the most significant ways you can involve service users is to find genuine ways of seeking their feedback on your practice. In the next section we will help you to plan ways of getting authentic feedback from service users about your work with them and the services they receive.

Service user feedback

You may be required to include service user feedback within your placement portfolio or other assessed work. Even if this is not an essential requirement, it is good practice in most settings and will certainly help you to develop your practice. As with any documents and materials other than those used within your agency, feedback must not reveal the identity of the service user or carer.

The experience of giving feedback

In order to continue to keep the service user at the centre of your practice, it is important to think about what the experience of giving feedback might mean for the people you are working with. Exercise 4.6 is a reflective task that will help you begin to think about how it might feel to be a service user giving feedback to a social worker.

If you were able to identify an occasion when your feedback was *not* listened to, you will recognise what a disempowering experience this can be. You therefore need to plan carefully how you will explain:

☑ **Why** service user feedback is important to you

☑ **What** will happen to any feedback given

☑ **How** it will be anonymised

☑ **Who** will see or hear any feedback that is given

Exercise 4.6   Giving feedback

Think about an experience you have had as a service user or consumer. For example, you could use your current experience as a student in college or university.

Think about a time when your feedback was both listened to and acted on

What happened?

_____

_____

_____

_____

How did you feel?

_____

_____

_____

_____

Think about a time when your feedback was not listened to or acted on

What happened?

_____

_____

_____

_____

How did you feel?

_____

_____

_____

_____

Even with careful planning and explanation, there are other factors which may impact on the extent to which service users feel comfortable and able to comment on your practice. The list below suggests some barriers that might get in the way of genuine feedback. People's responses will vary, of course – the important thing is to recognise that giving feedback may not be as straightforward as it seems. You need to think critically about the issues that could arise for the people you are working with and find ways of having conversations with them that are as open and honest as they can be. Some potential barriers are:

- fear of hurting your feelings or 'getting you into trouble'
- wanting to be liked by you
- fear of losing the service or not being allocated a new social worker
- anxiety that they will be known or recognised by people outside the agency who might read their comments.

It is important to recognise these thoughts and feelings and to find ways of addressing them if the feedback you are to receive is to be honest and authentic.

Getting feedback

It is really important to think about the most appropriate way to get feedback from the service users you are working with. As we have already seen, this should be sensitive to their situation but effective in capturing their thoughts and feelings.

You need to find methods of gaining feedback from service users that are appropriate to their age, abilities and preferences. For example, some people with learning difficulties may be able to give you meaningful feedback using a system of signs and symbols. Children may draw their feedback for you or enjoy using charts and stickers. An older person with dementia or someone with an illness or physical impairment may prefer to talk to you or to your supervisor rather than giving written feedback.

Remember ... some people may choose not to give you feedback and this needs to be respected.

Exercise 4.7 gives you an opportunity to think about how you will go about getting feedback from those you are working with on placement.

Signs and signals: feedback through action

Actions can often demand to be recognised and understood as much as verbal feedback. As a social worker you need to be responsive to verbal *and* non-verbal feedback. We sometimes refer to acts of *commission* (what people do) and acts of *omission* (what people don't do). If someone is angry and says so, this is very clear feedback. However, a service user missing appointments or constantly being late can also be a powerful message to the social worker.

Here are some examples:

- *When someone says 'thank you', or that they will miss you or that they are angry with you.*

This is feedback in itself. You might want to record these moments and reflect on them in supervision.

Exercise 4.7	Service user feedback action plan		
Action plan			
Who? (Group? Individual? Carer?)	How?	Possible barriers	Ways of overcoming barriers

- *A carer misses a number of pre-arranged meetings with you.*

If this happens you need to ask yourself why and what you can do to address the situation. For example, there may be practical reasons to do with transport or other commitments. Alternatively, this service user might not feel comfortable with your approach or with the approach of your agency.

- *A young person is always early for appointments at your office and is often waiting for you for a long time in reception.*

Again, there are a number of possible practical and emotional explanations for this, but it might be that s/he is quite dependent on you or perhaps that s/he does not feel safe at home.

Exercise 4.8 will help you to explore the issues involving feedback through actions.

Receiving feedback through actions

Think of some examples from your current placement or from past work or placement experiences where you have received feedback through actions (or non-actions) rather than in spoken or written form.

Example:

_____

_____

_____

_____

_____

_____

Example:

_____

_____

_____

_____

_____

_____

Finally, try to see negative as well as positive feedback as something helpful. If you can acknowledge criticism and reflect honestly with yourself on why it has been given, the chances are that this will lead to real improvements in your practice.

Service user participation and social work values

It is important to place service user participation in the context of your developing professional social work values. This will help you to relate the work you are undertaking (and service users' experience of that work) with the professional ethics involved in intervening in people's lives.

Exercise 4.9 **Feedback and values**

Use the spaces below to outline your plans for participation within the context of the core social work values as expressed in the Code of Practice for Social Care Workers (General Social Care Council 2002). Go back to the models discussed earlier in the chapter, to help you think about how you will promote participation within your individual practice.

Protect the rights and promote the interests of service users and carers

Example: In my work with carers I will speak with carers' groups to try to understand more about carers' concerns.

How will you *do this?*

_____

_____

_____

_____

Strive to establish and maintain the trust and confidence of service users and carers

Example: In my work with adults with learning difficulties I will be realistic in what my agency can provide. I cannot build and maintain trust if I break promises.

How will you *do this?*

_____

_____

_____

_____

_____

Promote the independence of service users while protecting them as far as possible from danger and harm

How will you do this?

_____

_____

_____

_____

_____

_____

Uphold public trust and confidence in social care services

How will you do this?

_____

_____

_____

_____

_____

_____

Be accountable for the quality of their work and take responsibility for maintaining and improving their knowledge and skills

How will you do this?

_____

_____

_____

_____

_____

_____

_____

Finally ...

You may not feel that your actions can make much difference to the inclusion of service users. However, this chapter has shown that it is important to 'do the small things well' (Laming 2003). Even as a student on placement you can play your part in helping to promote service user participation and involvement by keeping service users central to your learning by:

- Remembering the three models of participation (the Ladder, the Bridge, and the Hub and Spoke) to help you understand the complexities of service user participation.
- Applying the Service User Question to keep service users in mind and central to your practice.
- Finding different ways of seeking and receiving service user feedback.
- Linking social work values and service user participation.

Further reading and resources

J. Dalrymple and B. Burke, *Anti-Oppressive Practice: Social Care and the Law* (Maidenhead: Open University Press, 2006). This book has a helpful chapter on service user involvement, which includes lots of case examples.

www.shapingourlives.org.uk/index.html is a national service user network, which seeks to promote the voices of users of welfare services.

4

5 Making the most of supervision

This chapter will help you to ...

- **Understand what formal supervision is**
- **Organise supervision including keeping records**
- **Use informal supervision to help you on placement**
- **Work together with your supervisor to pass your placement**

66 The supervisor needs to make time for you to be supervised as a student and not only as a worker. You need to be able to talk about your development as a student.

DOMINIC *second-year student*

66 Remember, your learning is your responsibility too, and it's not just the practice educator.

NAS *third-year student*

Good supervision can make for a great placement, but if you have never worked in social care before you may wonder what it is and why it happens. If you've taken part in supervision before you may be looking for a different experience now you are undertaking your social work training. This chapter will help you prepare for supervision as a social work student and, as Dominic and Nas suggest, make sure you know how to establish clear roles and responsibilities throughout the process.

What is supervision?

Supervision is a time when you meet with your practice educator and/or workplace supervisor to talk in detail about your work on placement. Supervision plays a vital part in helping you to develop your professional identity. The purpose and process of arrangements may vary in different countries but in this chapter we refer to the UK supervisory social work context. (In this chapter the term 'supervisor' refers to the person who you have supervision with, which will always be your practice educator but may separately include a workplace supervisor or other colleague.) Supervision should happen on a regular basis, usually weekly or fortnightly, throughout the placement. It is usually one-on-one time, but sometimes students also take part in group supervision. Supervision is an important part of the placement as it gives you a regular opportunity to discuss how you are managing your work and developing towards becoming a professional social worker.

Colleges and universities expect your supervisor to offer you regular supervision sessions (check your college or university guidance for details). Although responsibility for organising and undertaking supervision is shared between you and your supervisor, it is a key responsibility of your supervisor to ensure that he or she is able to offer you supervision. This may mean them making sure that other work does not get in the way.

As you will see below, one of the key purposes of supervision is to contribute to your development and this will only happen if your supervisor uses their knowledge and skills, through supervision, to enable you to develop.

As a student, the way that supervision should be offered to you will not be the same as for other workers in the agency. You may find that you are getting more frequent supervision than other staff. This is because supervision as a social work student is central to your learning and its importance should be prioritised from the beginning of your placement.

The four functions of supervision

A useful way of thinking about supervision is to look at four functions of good supervision :

- workload
- development
- assessment
- support

Supervision can have many other functions within an agency and combining these functions is the key to giving and receiving good supervision (Hawkins and Shohet 2007).

As a social work student the 'development', i.e., educational, element is likely to be emphasised so that you are encouraged to consider issues such as social work values, professional identity and inter-professional working. Assessment will also be important and further details about this can be found in the next chapter, *Being assessed*.

If all four aspects are covered in your supervision session you are likely to feel that it has been helpful and constructive; Table 5.1 has more detail.

Table 5.1 The four functions of supervision

Functions	Description
Workload: managing the work you are doing	Your supervisor is accountable for your work and needs to help you to prepare for doing it. This will mean talking in detail about the work that you are doing. Much of it may be new to you. You will need to check how to get started and that what you are doing is okay. You will want to plan for what comes next.
	Through the work you do, you will show that you can be reliable and meet deadlines. You will be working with vulnerable people, often in a position of relative power and authority, so you will want to think about how to keep service users central and how to work in an anti-oppressive way.
Development: helping you to learn	Your learning needs to be put into a context of social work theory, knowledge, skills and values.
	Use supervision to discuss what you are learning from your work. This doesn't only mean making links with your reading and research from university; previous work and life experiences will also help you to develop your understanding. Through talking about how you understand service users' situations, your supervisor will be able to help you to develop your knowledge and understanding of the law, policy and social work values. This will help you to work out what type of intervention will be most effective.
	Part of assessing your work is to see whether you can use knowledge and learning from university in your day-to-day work. It is through doing this that you will develop the skills to make professional judgements and decisions.

5

Table 5.1 cont'd

Functions	Description
Assessment: getting feedback on your progress	Assessment is an important part of the placement. As a student you will be looking for regular feedback on how you are doing and whether you are starting to meet the occupational standards (see Chapter 6, *Being assessed*). You will find it helpful to set a regular time in supervision when you discuss your progress, the evidence you are collecting for your assessment, and any issues you need to work on or improve. In this way you will be able to participate actively in the assessment of your work rather than feeling that it is only the view of your practice educator that counts. It is a good idea to discuss specific pieces of work you are doing with service users in supervision so that your work is regularly reviewed.
Support:	Undertaking a social work placement is a rewarding but demanding experience. You may find that some of the work you do with service users affects you emotionally and challenges your own world view. You will have to think about the impact of who you are – your age, ethnic origin, gender, life experiences, and other factors – so that you can understand your emotional responses to your work. Supervision is a time to discuss these issues and learn how to develop your own professional strategies for coping with the challenges of practice. A good, trusting relationship with your supervisor will help you to feel able to do this.

Organising supervision

Planning

Good planning is important if supervision is to be effective and take place regularly. If you are in a busy placement and your practice educator has many demands on their time, you may need to help to ensure that supervision is well organised and meets your needs as a social worker in training. Table 5.2 lists some tips that will help you.

Supervisors have different levels of experience and students have different needs, but creating a clear framework for how supervision will be organised is a vital step towards getting what you need.

I found my best supervisions were when I took the lead and I said this is what I want to talk about … and I really got a lot out of that.

SAMERA *second-year student*

You should come away from supervision feeling informed and energised so that you can do your work well.

Table 5.2 Good practice in supervision

Good practice	Tips
Plan in advance	Arrange the dates for supervision and put them in your diary. You might schedule sessions for the whole placement or just the next few sessions.
Regular meetings	If a supervision session needs to be postponed, an alternative date for *that* session should be made.
Use a private space	Avoid any interruptions, such as colleagues popping in or answering phones.
Prepare well	Think in advance about what you want to get out of each supervision session (see Exercise 5.1).
Agree an agenda	Do this at the start of each session so that you get the chance to talk about what you need to.
Accurate records	This is important so that both you and your supervisor are clear about what you have discussed and decided, and what you have agreed needs to be done next.

Try completing Exercise 5.1 to help you think about what you are likely to need from supervision.

Carol is on a statutory placement, with a learning difficulties team, in her third year of training. Read Carol's plan for what she needs to learn from supervision and then think about your own learning needs.

Workload: I want to do a good job, so I need to know how to:
- introduce myself to service users
- carry out assessments and complete paperwork
- get to know other professionals working in the area and find out about services
- improve my skills in different ways of communicating with service users

What are *your* needs?

_____

_____

_____

_____

_____

Development: I need to know about:
- the legal rights of people with learning difficulties and their carers
- the social model of disability
- how stigma and discrimination affect the lives of people
- how to understand vulnerability and keeping people safe

What are *your* needs?

_____

_____

_____

_____

_____

5

Assessment: My confidence is more likely to increase if I know how I am getting along and that I am doing a good job. So I need to:

- ask my supervisor to give me regular feedback
- take work to supervision and try to make the links with the NOS

What are *your* needs?

_____

_____

_____

_____

Support: Statutory social work, and working with people with learning difficulties, is completely new to me. I need to be able to let my supervisor know that:

- I feel a bit overwhelmed
- I'm worried I won't be accepted by service users' families because people will think I am too young to do the job

What are *your* needs?

_____

_____

_____

_____

When you have finished thinking about your learning needs, try to move on to think about some of the ways in which they might be met.

Sometimes students worry that their supervisor hasn't previously worked with a student and that their supervision sessions might not be very productive. Some practice educators will have more experience than others, but as workers they will probably have experienced both good and bad supervision in their careers. They will want to work

with you to make your placement a success and should have a commitment to getting it right.

It is also very important to think about what you bring to supervision in terms of your existing knowledge, skills and experience. Exercise 5.2 prompts you to do this.

Exercise 5.2	Your existing knowledge and experience

Reflect on and identify relevant existing knowledge and experience in relation to:

Your previous experience through college, work and life

_____

_____

_____

Your knowledge about social care, communities and society

_____

_____

_____

Your skills that help you get along with people

_____

_____

_____

Your personal values and beliefs

_____

_____

_____

_____

Supervision agreement

In most placement settings, arrangements for supervision will be discussed at the beginning of your placement as part of your Practice Learning Agreement (see Chapter 2, *Learning for practice*). This

will set out the broad expectations of how you and your practice educator will be working together but it is also good practice to write a specific supervision agreement. This means you and your practice educator will need to talk in detail about how supervision will work: about aims, structure, functions, expectations and confidentiality (see Box A). A supervision agreement, setting ground rules, can help you to feel more confident about how to make the best of supervision.

Box A | Supervision agreement

Your supervision agreement should include:

- **Aims and purpose of supervision:** how supervision will help you to do good work and develop as a professional social worker during placement.
- **Practical arrangements:** where, when, agendas, time-keeping and recording .
- **The four functions of supervision:** how your workload management, development, assessment and support needs will be met.
- **Expectations of each other:** e.g., the need for honesty and openness, opportunities for discussion, learning, support, challenge, feedback and assessment.
- **Confidentiality:** the limits and boundaries of confidentiality, what it means for you and your service users.
- **Difficulties:** what to do if you or your supervisor have concerns about the supervisory process that you can't appear to resolve between you.

Supervision records

It is very important to keep supervision records for future reference; Table 5.3 explains why.

Table 5.3 Why keep records?

If you do keep records	If you don't …
All the work that you have done can be recorded. The notes can clearly state what work you need to do next and what your supervisor has agreed to do for next time	It will be hard to remember what you covered in the sessions and what you are meant to be doing next
Records show how you are learning and developing. For example, how you use your knowledge/reading etc. to help you to work better	Lots of your learning will go unrecorded
Records can provide useful evidence for your assessment	You could find yourself searching for evidence of your competence and you won't have a record of what you have achieved
Records can be very important in the case of disagreements between you and your supervisor about how you are getting on	There will be nothing to show whether or not you have been properly supported by your supervisor

Who writes the notes?

It is also important to decide who will write up the supervision notes. Often, supervisors will do this, but you need to agree that the content accurately reflects what *you* think happened in the session. You may be asked to, or want to, write up supervision notes. This can be a good learning experience and let you feel a more equal partner in the supervision process. Often supervisor and student alternate the recording of supervision sessions. It is always helpful if supervision notes are produced promptly and are signed by both supervisor and student to indicate their accuracy.

What is recorded on supervision notes?

Your supervision notes need to document, in summary, what was discussed in supervision and should broadly cover the four functions of supervision (see Table 5.4). Your university handbook may include a pro forma for the recording of supervision which your university requires you to use.

Group supervision

In some placement settings, *group* supervision may be offered. It is a group setting for undertaking the supervisory process and you can benefit from having support from, and learning with, other colleagues. The circumstances and arrangements for this will vary from agency to agency. For example, it might be that you are one of several students on placement in the agency, or you may be drawn together from a number of different agencies. In some circumstances a practice educator or supervisor may be supervising several

Table 5.4 Recording the four functions of supervision

Functions	What to record
Workload	Current activity and future expectations.
Development	Analysis of work you have done, how your knowledge and understanding has impacted on your decision making, how you have used the social work codes of practice and what issues you need to follow up and research further.
Assessment	Feedback on your supervisor's assessment of your progress, planning future assessment, links with the National Occupational Standards.
Support	How you are you feeling about your placement and the work you are doing. Brief record of any personal issues affecting the placement and any additional support required.

students, who are all brought together for some supervision sessions. Alternatively, you may be brought together in relation to a particular topic by someone within the agency with a particular responsibility for practice learning.

Advantages of group supervision

Group supervision can be an immensely helpful way of:

- sharing your learning
- reflecting on a range of different practice experiences
- engaging with a range of perspectives
- finding out about different resources, training and shadowing opportunities
- finding mutual support

It is, however, just as important within the group as within individual supervision sessions to ensure that the individual learning needs you identified above are met. Your supervision agreement should relate to group supervision as well as to any individual sessions that are planned. It will also be helpful to ensure that ground rules are agreed at an early stage so that you and the rest of the group can get as much benefit as possible from your time together.

Undertaking your placement in your own agency

> "They need to change their expectations of you. You are now a student but your manager may want you to carry on doing the work you have done and you are not there to do that. You are there as a student to learn and your supervision needs to reflect this.
>
> PHIL *second-year student*

If you are in this situation it can be particularly difficult to get the right sort of supervision. Unless you are proactive, supervisors may just continue with the form of supervision you had before you started your training and not fully recognise your new role.

As Phil notes, just as your role needs to change, so does the supervision that you require. In this respect you should be treated as a student who is new to the team and given the appropriate supervision focused on your needs as a trainee social worker. It is a good idea to talk with your manager and colleagues, before the placement starts, to make sure they understand your new role (Chapter 1, *Getting started*, includes some specific ideas about how you might do this). If you find that you are not receiving the right kind of supervision then talk with your university tutor as soon as possible.

Working with practice educators and workplace supervisors

Placements can be organised in a variety of different ways and you may be on a placement where you are working with a practice educator (who is 'off site', i.e., does not work in your office or practice base) and a workplace supervisor (who is 'on site', i.e., works at your office or practice base). Check your university handbook to make sure you understand their respective roles and that this is clearly set out in the Practice Learning Agreement.

Working with two supervisors will mean you will have a variety of support and experience to draw on for your learning. Table 5.5 identifies some of the issues that can sometimes arise when working with two supervisors.

Informal supervision

There is formal and informal supervision and I think you need remember how important informal supervision is during the week. Otherwise you might not get time to discuss everything in one session.

Nas *third-year student*

We have been looking at 'formal' supervision, but much of the support and guidance you receive on a day-to-day basis is likely to come through informal contact with your practice educator or workplace supervisor. You will often find yourself looking for immediate advice, the chance to talk through ideas and for support there and then. People need to be available to you throughout the working week, not just during your allocated supervision slot. This probably won't only be your supervisor, but also your colleagues in the workplace. It can be hard for one supervisor to provide you with everything that you need so working with others can be really helpful and they will also give you different points of view.

You will need to ask questions and consult at every stage of your placement, particularly in the early

Table 5.5 Working with two supervisors

Things that might concern you	Tips
I don't know who to go to for what	Make sure the roles are clear and you know who does what. The best time to do this is when you negotiate your Practice Learning Agreement
I'm getting mixed messages from my practice educator and workplace supervisor about what I should be doing	Let your supervisors know this is happening – so that they can work better together
My workplace supervisor and practice educator don't seem to be talking to each other	They need to build in more communication. Ask them to let you know how often they will be in touch with each other and issues they will discuss
I'm not sure who is the more important for my placement. It feels as if I need to try harder for my assessor	If you are clear about their roles you will be able to understand how to work in a way that meets their expectations and aids your learning
I don't know how well I am doing on placement	Ask them how they are going to make sure you get the feedback you need so that you can do the work well
I don't know which of them is responsible for assessing me	Talk to each of them about how they will contribute to your assessment: who will do the direct observations or complete placement reports?
I feel like I'm stuck in the middle	Ask to revisit your Practice Learning Agreement to clarify everyone's roles. See Chapter 8, *Troubleshooting*

Here are some ideas that may work for you, add some of your own too ...

- Arrange a regular 'check-in time' with your supervisor – at the beginning of the placement this may be on a daily basis – so that you know when s/he is going to be available
- Ask your supervisor to be upfront when s/he is pushed for time or under pressure. When you have an urgent query yourself, it is easy to miss the pressures on others
- Agree on who you should approach if your supervisor is busy. If the advice you get conflicts with that given previously by your practice educator, check it out again in supervision
- Agree about where decisions made through informal supervision contact will be recorded

Your ideas

days, and it is good practice to do so. If you observe your colleagues you will see that even the most experienced staff talk through their work with colleagues. As the placement goes along, you will find that you build on your experience and become more able to act with confidence and autonomy.

Ground rules for informal supervision

It can help to have some ground rules about informal supervision, so that your practice educator will be able to let you know if s/he is busy and you need to come back later or approach another colleague in the workplace. Exercise 5.3 will help you to think about what the ground rules should be in your particular placement.

Working together

From the moment that you first meet your supervisor, you are likely to be wondering whether you will get on well. The relationship between you and your supervisor is important in terms of how much you will learn from and enjoy your placement. The sort of working relationship that develops between the two of you will be seen most strikingly during supervision. If things are going well, you will feel that your needs are being addressed and you are able to:

☑ get on well with the work that is expected of you
☑ perform to the best of your ability in your assessment

☑ discuss your achievements and concerns in an open and supportive way

☑ learn from the work you are doing

☑ acknowledge mistakes

If this is happening, you are then likely to find that supervision is productive and enjoyable. It is also worth noting that supervision will change over time as you develop and your needs change. You may well find yourself feeling a greater sense of equality with your practice educator towards the end of your final placement.

Power dynamics in supervision

Your supervisor is, in some respects, more powerful than you in the context of the supervisor/ supervisee relationship. S/he will be required to make judgements about your work and play an important part in the decision about whether you pass or fail your placement. This may not feel a comfortable position to be in, particularly if the assessment process feels continuous throughout your placement.

Specific issues may arise around themes such as gender, ethnicity, sexuality and disability, which will contribute to the power dynamics within the supervisory relationship. As you develop your own professional views, values and identity you will be able to work with these issues in an appropriate and constructive way in supervision and in your practice (see the section 'Social Work Values' in Chapter 6, *Being assessed*).

It is worth remembering that often supervisors don't feel very powerful themselves. They too have hopes and aspirations that your placement will go well and that you will develop your skills appropriately. Yet they may be new to the role of practice educator, and be grappling with the complexities of your university's assessment requirements whilst also juggling their existing workload.

Occasionally, within a supervisory relationship, supervisors may exercise their power inappropriately. This may be done in an intentionally covert or overt way, or it may be unintentional due to their limited experience in the practice educator's role. If this happens it can make you feel unsure of yourself, intimidated, undermined, deskilled or even bullied or oppressed.

If this happens to you, think about how you want to address the issues. Many of the ideas in this book for seeking advice and support involve you being assertive and raising issues with your supervisor, but in this situation you may need to call on others to help. You may feel you can't talk to your supervisor directly about these issues and need to contact your college tutor for support. Chapter 8, *Troubleshooting*, provides further guidance about this.

Using feedback

Regular feedback is a really important part of your placement. You need to know how you are getting on, what you are doing well and how you need to develop. If you don't feel that you know how you are progressing on placement make sure that you ask in supervision.

> **Remember ...**
> positive *and* negative feedback are *both* useful for your professional development.

Getting complimentary feedback will boost your confidence and energy levels. It is really important that you find out what you are doing well, so learn to enjoy this sort of feedback. Try to make sure that you find out what precisely it is that is successful, so that you can apply this learning in other situations.

Think about how you feel about giving and receiving feedback because you are going to be asking service users to give you feedback; remember, they may find it makes them feel uncomfortable too. Reading the section 'Service User Feedback' in Chapter 4 may help you explore these ideas further.

Receiving constructive criticism or 'negative feedback' may not sound like a pleasant experience. However, the important point to remember is that the feedback is aimed at helping you to improve and develop. Constructive criticism is not about criticising you as an individual but is rather aimed at giving you an understanding of how to approach practice situations in the future. There is rarely one right answer in social work and reflecting on your practice, and having others comment on it, is part of the professional role. Exercise 5.4 on the following page will help you reflect on the experience of receiving negative feedback and enable you to recognise that this is part of your development rather than something to be taken personally.

Disappointment and difficulties

Students often have very high hopes for their placement and high expectations of their supervisor. You may find that things just don't measure up but you will still need to complete your placement and use supervision in this process. The important thing is to be sure that your supervision is 'good enough'. You may find that there are some changes you can bring about, as well as perhaps adapting your own expectations. Your supervisor needs to know how you are feeling and that you want to do things differently.

Sometimes supervisory relationships do break down and it is not productive for either you or your supervisor to continue meeting. The reason this happens varies but often relates to a clash of personalities or fundamental difference of opinion about a placement issue. If you feel you are in this situation, remember you are able to challenge the

5

Exercise 5.4 | Receiving negative feedback

Think about a time when you received negative feedback about something:

How did it make you feel?

_____

_____

_____

Did it seem fair?

_____

_____

_____

How did you take the criticisms on board and change?

_____

_____

_____

How long did it take you to do this?

_____

_____

_____

How might the feedback have been given to be more constructive?

_____

_____

_____

How might you react differently to constructive criticism in the future?

_____

_____

_____

views and assumptions of your supervisor. It is okay to disagree and to seek support from your university tutor.

Chapter 8, *Troubleshooting*, gives further advice about things you can do in this situation.

Finally ...

Supervision is an important part of a successful placement. This chapter has looked at how to get the most out of supervision by:

- Understanding what supervision is.
- Introducing the four functions of supervision.
- Helping you to organise effective supervision.
- Helping you to think about your relationship with your supervisor.

Good supervision will help you make sure that you learn effectively on placement and develop towards becoming a professional social worker.

Further reading and resources

J. Knapman and T. Morrison, *Making the Most Out of Supervision – a Self-Development Manual for Supervisees* (Brighton: Pavilion, 2004). This is one of the few texts written for students rather than the supervisors.

J. Parker, *Effective Practice Learning in Social Work* (Exeter: Learning Matters, 2004). See the student-focused chapter 'Using supervision to enhance practice learning and practice competence'.

6   Being assessed

This chapter will help you to ...

- **Think about the role of assessment in your placement**
- **Work with your practice learning team**
- **Understand how to collect and present evidence of your work**

---

66 Finding the time to do my portfolio work was really hard. I needed to show the work I was doing and this required evidence.

EVE *third-year student*

66 Thanks to my practice educator I got organised from day one and made sure that I kept my university tutor involved too.

ELLEN *second-year student*

Stop for a minute. Think how much is asked of you on placement. It's like starting a new job but as well as settling in, developing your social work skills and trying to help service users, you are also going to be assessed. As Eve and Ellen note, you will need to manage both your work with service users and the requirements of your course to demonstrate your competence. This chapter is going to help you find ways to make your assessed placement a success. Firstly, we discuss how social work practice is assessed in the UK and then consider key meetings and different people's roles on placement. Secondly, we look at collecting evidence of your work, which you will use to show that you have developed your social work skills. The last part of this chapter looks at what to do if you are having difficulties passing your placement, and who can help you.

Assessment

What is assessment?

In the UK assessment is the way you can demonstrate that you have met the standard required to become a professional social worker. All courses in the UK that train students to be professional social workers use a competency-based approach. This means you have to provide evidence to indicate that you are working to a good enough standard, i.e., that you are competent to be a social worker. In the UK this will mean that, amongst other skills, you will have developed an analytical approach to your social work practice and will have the ability to be critically reflective of the work you do. You will need to show that you are an accountable and responsible practitioner. The competency-based approach makes the assessment process as fair as possible. In other words, you don't just pass because your practice educator likes you; you pass because you demonstrate you can do the job.

Not many people like being tested or assessed but it is the fairest way to establish whether someone has developed their skills and knowledge sufficiently to meet the required standard. Being assessed can be stressful.

Remember ... you are being assessed to the level of a first-, second- or third-year student social worker – not an experienced, qualified social worker.

After all, you have probably invested a lot of your time, money and energy in your training, so not passing may have consequences beyond simple disappointment (see Chapter 7, *Managing stress on placement*, for some useful tips). However, by taking the opportunities presented to you during your placement you should be able to achieve a pass by demonstrating your developing social work skills.

How is social work practice assessed?

In England, Wales and Northern Ireland the current criteria that your developing knowledge and skills for social work practice are assessed against are the National Occupational Standards (NOS) for Social Work issued by the care councils of each nation or region. The occupational standards describe 21 units of competence, which are grouped together into six key roles (see Box A). The equivalent Scottish criteria are the Standards in Social Work Education (see Appendix B). In this book the term 'occupational standards' is used to encompass both the Scottish and the other UK-wide standards. These standards are often part of a wider policy framework for social work education.

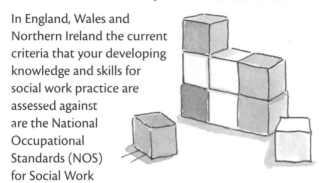

These occupational standards have been developed to create a framework of core skills that a social worker in training should be able to demonstrate at a level appropriate to the stage of their training. Your placement is a learning experience, not a work experience (Doel and Shardlow 2005).

By setting standards, the government aims to ensure its workforce has the right skills and knowledge to meet the needs of service users, carers and communities. The occupational standards are the building blocks of your placement. That is, as you spend more time on placement working with colleagues, carers and

Box A	The National Occupational Standards for Social Work in England, Wales and Northern Ireland

Key Role 1: Prepare for, and work with, individuals, families, carers, groups and communities to assess their needs and circumstances

Key Role 2: Plan, carry out, review and evaluate social work practice with individuals, families, carers, groups, communities and other professionals

Key Role 3: Support individuals to represent their needs, views and circumstances

Key Role 4: Manage risk to individuals, families, carers, groups, communities, self and colleagues

Key Role 5: Manage and be accountable, with supervision and support, for your own social work practice within your organisation

Key Role 6: Demonstrate professional competence in social work practice

service users you will begin using the occupational standards to shape, develop and focus your practice. Your training is aimed to help you to develop your professional identity as a social worker, and understanding the core skills and social work values your professional role will demand is part of this process.

Occupational standards are broadly defined so that they can be applied to a variety of tasks in varied practice settings. They are also rigorous enough to establish an academic benchmark for the standards of professional practice. You and your practice educator will have to read and discuss the occupational standards to agree what each unit and key role means in your particular practice setting. For example, in England, NOS 1, Unit 3,

'Assess needs and options to recommend a course of action', may be interpreted differently depending on whether you are working in a statutory childcare team or whether you are working in a residential home for people with learning difficulties.

The style in which occupational standards are written and the fact that there are a lot of them can be daunting to begin with. However, don't be put off: look at Exercise 6.1 and use the descriptions in the key roles and units to help you match the work you are doing with what you need to demonstrate to pass the placement.

Social work values

You will also have to demonstrate that your practice follows social work's *professional values*. On your placement you may hear colleagues talking about their social work values and many will agree that professional social work practice is based on a strong value base.

However, from a student perspective, identifying the profession's values is not straightforward as there is no single statement of what social work's professional values are for the UK. The codes of practice issued by the social care councils for England, Scotland, Wales and Northern Ireland give some guidance. The occupational standards also suggest the values that student social workers must demonstrate (see Box B for some examples). Remember to make sure you know how your university wants you to show that you are working within social work values and which statement of professional values they refer to (see Chapter 1, *Getting started*).

Exercise 6.1 Occupational standards

Think of a piece of work you have done on placement and identify two key roles that it might relate to.

Example

Lucy: "I spent an afternoon last week undertaking a carer's assessment with the husband of a lady who has Alzheimer's disease. I think I met several of the National Occupational Standards, including Key Role 1 Unit 2 (work with individuals … to help them make informed decisions) as a lot of our conversations were about me helping the carer to understand the extra support available to him at home. I also think I met Key Role 4 (managing risk) because I undertook an assessment of the risks to both the carer (and his wife) of him carrying on providing 24 hour care by himself."

Piece of work:

_____

_____

_____

_____

First key role:

_____

_____

_____

_____

Second key role:

_____

_____

_____

_____

- Show awareness of your own values, prejudices, ethical dilemmas and conflicts
- Value, recognise and respect the diversity, expertise and experience of individuals, families, carers, groups and communities
- Understand, and make use of, strategies to challenge discrimination, disadvantage and other forms of inequality and injustice

(National Occupational Standards (England) Key Role 1, Unit 3)

It is important that you reflect upon the influence of your values and prejudices on your social work practice and learn to incorporate the profession's value base into your work.

Statutory tasks and contrasting placements

In setting the standards of social work education the UK care councils make some other requirements of placements. In England, Scotland and Northern Ireland one requirement is that by the end of your training you must have had experience of **statutory tasks involving legal interventions**. A 'statutory social work task' is something a social worker *must do or has the power to do* as a result of a particular piece of legislation. You will be assessed on undertaking this type of task during at least one of your placements (see Box C for examples of statutory social work tasks). In Wales a distinct, but related requirement, is that one period of assessed practice must be undertaken within a local social services authority.

Box C	Examples of statutory tasks

Contributing to a
- Community Care assessment
- Mental Health Act assessment
- Court report

A second requirement for all UK social work students is that they must have experience of providing services to at least **two different service user groups**. If one placement is with older adults with mental health problems and the second placement is with a child support team this will be easy to achieve. If you are not clear whether you are being offered placements that give you the right contrasting experience, make sure you talk with the person responsible for organising your placements, probably your university tutor (or agency representative if you are a seconded/employed student). You will be assessed on your ability to work with different service user groups and you will have to develop different skills and knowledge to work with them effectively.

Remember, in addition to the outline information provided here, the four UK care councils will have made specific requirements regarding how your social work practice is to be assessed. For example, if you are studying in Wales you must demonstrate sensitivity to, as well as an awareness of, issues relating to the Welsh language. Make sure you consult your university guidelines, which should set out the specific requirements – drawn from the relevant care council's guidance – of what you must demonstrate during your period of assessed practice and how you must evidence it.

6

Placement people and structure

The practice learning team

Every university organises its placements differently but all will work with agencies offering social work placements. Universities and agencies aim to ensure that you have a placement where you can demonstrate your developing social work knowledge and skills. You and the key people represented in Box D are often called the practice learning team.

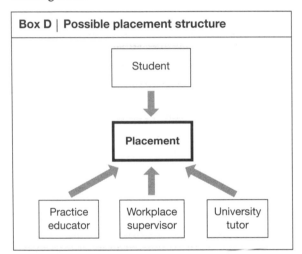

Box D | Possible placement structure

Student

↓

Placement

Practice educator — Workplace supervisor — University tutor

Depending on how your course is organised, the titles given to the different people involved in your placement might be different but the jobs they do will be similar. Below we consider the different roles.

Student

Without you there would be no placement and it is you who has to develop the skills and knowledge required to learn on placement. Other members of the team are going to help you but you have to be

an *active learner* seeking out opportunities for you to learn, develop and demonstrate why you should pass your placement. Part of this process will be engaging in critical reflection about your practice, in supervision, to enable you to develop your sense of identity as a professional social worker.

Practice educator

Practice educators have a dual role, both supporting and teaching you to develop your skills but also contributing to the assessment of whether you pass your placement. It is really important that you ask for feedback from your practice educator about how you are doing on placement.

Remember, not all practice educators will have worked with many students, or perhaps with students from your college or university, so try to develop a collaborative approach from the very beginning. Make sure both of you are clear about how your university wants you to evidence your work on placement. Be clear about what your practice educator is expecting of you and make sure he or she is in tune with how you are approaching your work.

Workplace supervisor

If your practice educator is not based at, or near, your placement then some courses organise a placement supervisor. This person will be based on or near your placement and is responsible more for your day-to-day needs. These include your induction programme and planning what work you will be doing. The placement supervisor will have a lesser role in the formal assessment of your practice but will work closely with your practice educator to ensure that your placement goes well. You may have supervision with both your practice educator and your workplace supervisor.

University tutor

The practice learning team will usually include a university tutor, or a person appointed by your university, to provide guidance and support on your placement. Typically, the university tutor will be involved in the key meetings during placement and will be keen to help you with applying university-based academic learning to your placement experience.

The balance of responsibility for the assessment of your work will vary between different social work training programmes. In some cases the practice educator may have considerable responsibility in determining whether a student will pass their placement; on other courses the university tutor may have more input. Make sure you understand how your course allocates these responsibilities between members of the practice learning team.

Key meetings

Below we summarise the types of meetings you may have during your placement with your practice learning team, and explain how to make them useful for you.

You may also find it useful to go back to Chapter 1, *Getting started*, which helps you to think about the early stages of placement and how you present yourself, while Chapter 2, *Learning for practice*, gives you some tools for thinking about your learning needs and the skills you bring to your placement.

Different social work training courses have different numbers and types of meetings during the course of the placements. Some placements will have an **Introductory Meeting**. The aim is to welcome you to the placement, usually to discuss your learning agreement and establish everybody's roles. In terms of *assessment* this meeting is important because you can:

- identify the key areas of experience you want to gain from the placement and what the placement can offer you
- identify the key skills you need to develop
- begin to consider how you can demonstrate your work to others in order to pass your placement.

If your course doesn't have a first meeting, don't worry. You will probably cover some of the above elements through email, telephone and individual face-to-face contact with your university tutor and practice educator.

Often courses will have an **Interim Meeting**. The purpose of the meeting is to:

- review your progress so far and let you know how well you are doing
- identify and make a plan to resolve any difficulties
- plan for the work you will do in the second part of your placement.

If you are having any difficulties on placement this is the meeting to make sure they are heard and noted. If you feel that you are doing good work but finding it hard to demonstrate how you are meeting the occupational standards, discuss this too. At the interim meeting, the level of your work may be formative rather than summative, but this is usually okay and what is expected at this stage at this stage (see Box E for an explanation). Remember, the standard or level of work you will be expected to demonstrate will vary depending on what stage of your training you are at.

Box E | Summative or formative work?

Formative work is done during the earlier stages of your placement as you begin to develop your knowledge and skills.

Summative work (leading to summative assessment) is when you are working at the required practice level for your placement and demonstrating this in the required way.

Almost all courses will have a **Final Meeting**. If your placement has gone well, this will focus on reviewing your successful placement and making sure that your work has been recognised through your university's assessment process. You may have had to produce a portfolio or select key pieces of work that will be used to assess your success on placement. If you have had difficulties on placement, the final meeting may be focused on a decision about whether you should pass your placement or not.

> **Remember ...**
> you can ask for an additional meeting with some or all members of the practice learning team if you feel this is needed.

Collecting evidence

What is evidence?

The idea of collecting 'evidence' maybe unfamiliar to you but it is central to your social work placement. An analogy is a detective collecting evidence of a crime (Parker 2004). The detective will hope that the evidence they collect will help to prove their case and convict the criminal in court. The evidence supports a particular view of events. Similarly, you will have to present evidence to other members of your practice learning team to prove *your case* that you have demonstrated your competence as a student social worker. The evidence you collect will be a central part of your regular discussions with your practice educator and, for your university tutor, it will mean they can see why your practice educator feels you are meeting the standard required.

Universities structure their social work courses differently and this will largely determine in what way you will have to collect and present evidence of your practice. Many courses require students to create a portfolio or file of evidence of their work. Other courses ask students to provide summaries of how they think they have met the occupational standards through a small sample of work attached to a practice educator's final report.

The occupational standards will be interpreted by those assessing you in the context of the stage of your training. A greater depth of evidence will be required for standards you are evidencing during a final placement than for your first placement.

The responsibility for gathering evidence is not just yours. Your practice educator has a responsibility for providing you with learning opportunities that will enable you to learn, develop your knowledge and skills, and to evidence this appropriately. One of your practice educator's roles will be to help you understand, and therefore make explicit, how a piece of social work practice might meet the occupational standards. This process can be straightforward or you might find that you have a different view to your practice educator regarding evidencing your work (see Chapter 5, *Making the most of supervision*, for guidance about establishing a productive working relationship with your practice educator, or Chapter 8, *Troubleshooting*, for guidance on how to resolve placement issues).

Below is a summary of the different ways of collecting evidence you are likely to use on your social work course. How you then present your evidence will vary from course to course.

Assessed observations of practice

Common to all social work courses in the UK is the need for you to have your social work practice observed. Your practice educator will normally be the person observing your work and usually the observation will be of you working directly with

service users. The aim is to see how your social work skills are developing, to assess how you are working towards meeting the occupational standards and to give the practice educator an opportunity to provide feedback to you.

Box F | Preparing for your direct observation

- Don't leave your direct observations too late – you may run out of time
- Identify a piece of work that will let you show your educator your knowledge and skills
- Gain service users' permission for your educator to be with you and explain that they may take notes
- Think about the piece of work you are going to do and jot some reminders to take with you

---

Social work is about working with people, so the development of your interpersonal skills, and also your specific social work skills, is a vital part of your placement experience. Direct observations of practice are the best way for you to show what you can do and for your practice educator to be able to provide you with suggestions and guidance. Direct observations require careful planning (see Box F) and students sometimes feel nervous beforehand. However, remember that you do not pass or fail a direct observation but receive feedback on your progress in developing your skills.

As Dominic notes below, not all direct observations have to be planned. You can take advantage of situations on placement, where unplanned observations take place, to help you demonstrate your skills and knowledge.

> *I was working on the duty desk when a service user came into reception. He was really distressed and I spent lots of time helping him find accommodation for the night. I was working with Phil, the Senior Practitioner, and he agreed to provide some feedback for me to include in my portfolio.*

DOMINIC *third-year student*

Service user and carer feedback

Service users and carers will have a unique perspective on your work and can provide valuable feedback. They will probably not be able to comment on the occupational standards but they will be able to say what it was like working with you. Finding a sensitive and appropriate way to document service user and carer feedback can in turn be a very effective way of demonstrating how you are meeting standards. Depending on the nature of the service users' difficulties you will need to use an appropriate way to gain feedback. This might include the use of short questionnaires, pictorial feedback or audio feedback and so on (Chapter 4 includes detail about how and why you should seek service user feedback).

Practice documents

> *I helped write a risk assessment with a service user returning home after being in hospital with depression. We looked at the risk of becoming low again and wrote a relapse prevention plan. This work fitted in with Key Role 4 Unit 12.*

EVA *second-year student*

Whatever your placement setting you will probably have the chance to complete some documentation relating to the work you are doing. In a residential home or day centre the majority of your work may be face to face with service users and practice documents will be less central to your work. In a statutory team practice documents, such as assessments, care plans and reviews, will probably be part of your everyday work. Properly anonymised, these documents can provide strong evidence of your practice. As Eva notes in the quote, her work on risk assessment helped her to evidence Key Role 4 Unit 12, 'Assess and manage risk to individuals, families, groups and communities'.

Reflective writing

Depending on the requirements of your course, you may be asked to complete a number of pieces of written work which, in essence, centre on your reflections of the work you are doing on placement.

As we saw in Chapter 2, *Learning for practice*, reflective practice focuses on how you develop your skills in thinking about the work you do. In the process of gathering evidence, engaging in a reflective process will help you identify pieces of work where you demonstrate your knowledge and skills. Exercise 6.2 prompts you to begin reflecting on your practice (Chapter 2 provides more detailed models and exercises to help you get to grips with reflection).

Other evidence from your placement

Other information you gather on placement that indicates the work you have been doing can also provide useful evidence for assessment. This

Think about the last piece of work you did with a service user ...

- What went well and how do you know this?

- Do you know what the service user thought about your work?

- What made the difference that resulted in the change?

- What could you have done differently to develop the outcome?

- What were the power dynamics of the situation?

could include evidence of project work, articles in newsletters, presentations you've given to the team, supervision notes or a reflective diary.

The type of setting in which you are undertaking your practice learning will influence which sources of evidence you will use. For example, if you are working in a statutory setting it is likely that there will be many practice documents – assessments, care plan reviews, letters – which you can use as evidence. If you are working in a non statutory residential setting, perhaps direct observations of your work with service users will be an easier way of gaining evidence. Alternatively, undertaking group work with users and carers may make it easy to gather their feedback about your work.

Collecting evidence

In the busyness of day-to-day working life it is important to develop your own system for collecting evidence of your work. Below are some suggestions that might help.

☑ **Start early:** don't wait for the big event; everyday work will create evidence you can use to show you are meeting the occupational standards.

☑ **Collect as you are going along:** it is much easier to collect evidence day by day (e.g., photocopying practice documents you complete) than it is to try to find those documents towards the end of your placement.

☑ **Use a variety of different types of evidence** from direct observation through to practice documents: different types of evidence will be more useful to you in meeting particular occupational standards.

☑ **Involve the people around you:** colleagues, service users, people from other agencies can all provide evidence of your work.

☑ **Make sure you don't include the names of service users or carers** in your evidence. If you are using practice documents make sure you blank out the users' and carers' names, date of births and addresses. You may have to photocopy the document once you've done this so that no names are visible when the document is held up to the light.

☑ **Make sure you are open and honest with service users:** let them know why you are asking for their feedback and that if they don't want to it's not a problem. Never give the impression that giving feedback is linked to whether somebody receives a service. See Chapter 4 for a detailed discussion about giving and receiving feedback. Remember, you must seek service users' consent before including their material as evidence.

☑ **Don't forget that your work is developing throughout the placement** and therefore earlier work may appear at a lower level than later work; this is okay. Your success will be influenced by how much you are able to develop your knowledge and skills on placement. You want to pass but the nature of learning is that you will make mistakes along the way and some pieces of your work will be stronger than others.

How do I know if my evidence is good enough?

It can be difficult to decide whether the evidence you are collecting, such as letters and user feedback, is good enough to help you meet the occupational standards or other assessment framework you are working with. It is important to be very clear about the assessment style of your university or college and how they want you to evidence your work at each level. Make sure you read your course guide on assessment and talk with your practice educator. You also need to ensure that you present your evidence in accordance with course guidelines using any templates or documents provided. Table 6.1 sets out six questions to ask yourself about evidence you want to use to demonstrate your work.

Table 6.1 Considering your evidence

Is your evidence ...	
Focused?	Does a piece of evidence demonstrate you are meeting a key role or units from the occupational standards? Is it linked to your practice learning objectives?
Enough?	Does a piece of evidence on its own show you have met a key role or unit? You may need several examples of your work to show your practice educator you have met a particular key role or unit.
Based on social work values?	Does it reflect anti-oppressive values and promote a value-based approach to social work?
Reliable?	Does the evidence build a consistent picture of your work when taken together with other evidence of your practice?
Clear?	It is often useful to think of a tutor or examiner who does not know you coming to read your work; they need to be able to understand the evidence you have presented and why you think it meets the occupational standards.
Agreed?	Have your practice educator, and others involved in the piece of work, agreed that it meets the units you are claiming?

Adapted from Parker (2004)

What if you think you might not pass your placement?

You may not pass your placement on the first attempt. Sometimes problems arise on placement that will be beyond your control but, in most cases, issues will arise if your social work practice does not meet the standard required.

If you feel that you are having difficulties on placement it is important that you seek support and help from your university tutor and practice educator. You need to establish what the difficulties are and consider what your next steps should be.

You may have found that social work practice is simply not what you expected and that it is not the right profession for you. While difficult and complicated at the time, this experience can lead to

a more appropriate course of study in the future. If you do decide social work is not for you, get some advice from your university about future study: the academic credits you may have already gained could count towards an alternative degree.

You may want to continue with your training but find that you are not able to meet the standards required to join the profession and will not be able to continue with your studies. This will be a difficult experience but, ultimately, social work training has to be primarily focused on ensuring that those who qualify and join the profession are appropriately skilled to work with service users and carers.

Alternatively you, like many students, may find that with the help of your practice educator and university tutor you can improve and develop your skills to the required standard and continue with your studies. It is not your responsibility alone to seek extra help; your practice educator and university tutor also need to use their skills and experience to enable you to progress. It is likely that they will know that you are struggling with your placement but make sure you talk to them as soon as you can. Together you can identify the key issues and make a plan to resolve them.

Finally ...

This chapter has focused on the assessment element of your placement. Working with the right people to support and develop your skills and knowledge during placement is really important for your success. You should now be able to:

- Understand the importance of the occupational standards in relation to passing your placement.
- Identify the practice learning team and key placement meetings.
- Start to collect evidence to support the work you do and make sure this is of a good standard and presented in the right way for your course.

Further reading and resources

J. Healey and M. Spencer, *Surviving Your Placement in Health and Social Care* (Maidstone: Open University Press, 2008). This general guide to placements will help you to consider the broad issues of assessment further.

J. Parker, *Effective Practice Learning in Social Work* (Exeter: Learning Matters, 2004). This book, which includes lots of helpful materials for students on placement, has a chapter on the assessment of practice learning, gathering evidence and demonstrating competence.

7 Managing stress on placement

This chapter will help you to ...

- **Understand stress**
- **Find out why placements can be stressful**
- **Prevent stress from building up**
- **Manage stress on placement**
- **Get extra help if you need to**

66 Once I'd worked out how to prioritise my work I felt less stressed about it all.

PHIL *second-year student*

66 Sometimes on placement you realise just how much work is being asked of you; it can feel really heavy.

YASMIN *first-year student*

7

As Yasmin notes, undertaking a placement involves a lot of hard work. Everyone is different, but most students on placement will find it stressful at some point. You may be concerned about how your placement is going, whether you are getting on well with your practice educator or whether the service users you are working with will be okay. Don't worry. Having these, and many other concerns, is usual and to be expected. What is important is to find a way of managing the work you have to complete and to manage the stress too.

This chapter will begin by looking at what stress is, so that you can learn to recognise if you are starting to experience high levels of stress. We then look at how placements can be stressful, how to identify the sources of stress while on placement and how to avoid, solve and manage the sources of stress. Finally, we offer some advice for accessing specialist help if needed.

By the end of the chapter you will have been introduced to some of the ways you can stay healthy, monitor your stress levels and take action to make stress work for you.

What is stress?

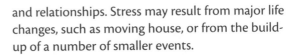

Stress is the experience of feeling that the demands put on you are greater than your ability to cope. Stress is caused by many different situations; the most common are linked to work, financial issues and relationships. Stress may result from major life changes, such as moving house, or from the build-up of a number of smaller events.

The experience of being stressed is very individual and what may be stressful for you will not necessarily be stressful for someone else. You will have coped with, literally, thousands of stressful events throughout your life but each day brings new combinations of events, which may push you to your own personal threshold for feeling 'stressed'.

The good news is that some stress can be good for you: it focuses your mind and produces biological changes in your body that can improve the way you work. What is important is that you learn to identify and manage your stress so that it does not become a problem.

Feeling stressed can result from there being:

- **too much stress at once:** there are just too many things to do, and to cope with stress like this you have to either reduce the number of things you are doing or find a way to manage the stress;
- **stress for too long:** the short-term stress response that gives you lots of energy does not work well in the longer term. You need to find a different way to cope (Cottrell 2007).

What changes occur in your body when you are stressed?

We all have an instinctive response to high levels of stress, often referred to as 'fight or flight'. When we were all hunter gatherers, and encountered danger from animals or other tribal groups, the fight or flight response is what kept us safe. Under threat the body releases hormones, such as adrenaline, which give a person the energy either to stay to fight off the threat or to run away.

The difficulty today is that the pace of modern life means 'fight or flight' hormones are stimulated by many daily situations but we do not get to use them effectively. For example, if your manager asks you to write a difficult report, which makes you feel stressed, it is not appropriate to start a fight or to run out of the office! So, as we cannot fight or run away the chemicals in our bodies do not get used and over time the changes they produce can damage your physical and mental health.

vs

What do you notice if you are starting to get stressed?

Firstly, watch out for **physical changes** in your body. These will be different for everyone but may include:

- disturbed sleep pattern – you can't get to sleep, stay asleep or get up from sleep
- high blood pressure – you may not notice this but if it's identified by your GP it may be linked to your stress levels
- headaches and muscle aches – back, neck and shoulders
- indigestion
- feeling sick and/or having stomach aches
- eating too much or too little

Equally important is the need to be aware of the **emotional changes** stress can cause. Watch out for:

- feelings of low self-esteem and that 'I just can't do it' feeling
- feeling low in mood and unhappy
- feeling irritable
- feeling anxious and overwhelmed

Finally, you may find yourself acting differently if you are feeling stressed. These are **behavioural changes** and might include:

- poor concentration and finding it difficult to focus on one single task
- confused thinking and difficulty making decisions
- increased use of alcohol, coffee, tobacco, prescribed and non-prescribed drugs
- spending less time with friends and family

Sometimes feeling stressed can be very short term, lasting only a day or two, if the cause of the stress is obvious and soon resolves itself. If you notice some of the physical, emotional and behavioural changes happening to you over a longer period of time, perhaps a week or so, then you need to take steps to look after yourself and manage the stress.

7

Why can placements be stressful?

Starting placement can be an exciting time. If you are new to social care it may be one of your first experiences of getting out into the workplace to develop your social work skills and meet service users. If you have worked in social care before then the placement is a chance to develop your skills further and begin to develop your identity as a professional social worker. However, don't forget that being on placement is, for even the most confident and able student, a very challenging time.

When you are on placement you will have to balance a number of new activities at the same time, as Figure 7.1 illustrates. It is likely to be the combination of having to undertake lots of new types of work, in a new environment, maybe away from your friends and family, which can lead to stress.

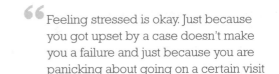

Feeling stressed is okay. Just because you got upset by a case doesn't make you a failure and just because you are panicking about going on a certain visit it doesn't mean you're not up to the job.

SAMERA *second-year student*

All these demands will be in addition to the other aspects of your life which you will have to continue to manage. You may, of course, find that personal events happen during your training such as a family bereavement, illness or pregnancy. You may find you are feeling stressed on placement but that the source of the stress is unrelated to your social work training. Your friends and family will also be adjusting to your developing skills and knowledge. Sometimes this can mean the nature of relationships change and tensions arise.

Avoiding stress

It is important to remember that you have some control over how stressful you find your placement. If you believe that you can influence the way life unfolds you will experience lower levels of stress than someone who believes that life just happens through luck or the actions of others. The placement you are undertaking is *your* placement; it has been created so that you can develop your social work skills. This section will look at how you can avoid unnecessary stress and work effectively. Plan well, look after yourself and you will increase your chances of having a good experience.

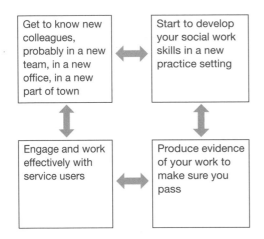

Figure 7.1 Balancing new activities

Looking after your basic needs

You will probably already be very good at looking after yourself but it is also important to recognise that continuing to take care of the basics will help you manage being on placement. Ask yourself the following questions:

- Am I eating well and regularly?
- Am I taking regular exercise?
- Am I trying to keep a regular sleep pattern?
- Do I have any 'me' time?
- Am I getting to spend a reasonable amount of time with friends and family?
- Am I drinking only moderate amounts of alcohol and caffeine?

If you answered 'no' to any of these questions then you may need to change your day-to-day routines so you have time to look after yourself better. If you don't look after yourself – in terms of diet, exercise, sleep and family life etc. – then you are likely to be less able to cope with any stressful events that come along on placement.

Looking after yourself on placement

At the start of your placement, or as soon as you've read this chapter, begin to make some changes to reduce the chances of you experiencing unhelpful levels of stress. For example, you could:

- **Identify sources of support** both within and outside the placement. This might be your practice educator, college or university tutor, friends or family.
- **Make sure you keep in touch with your friends** from the course for support. You may all have some similar challenges on placement and can support each other. You may feel isolated on placement if you have been used to meeting with other students regularly. Isolation can lead to stress.

- **Join or set up a support group.** Meeting up with colleagues to share experiences can be very helpful and you may pick up some tips on how to meet common placement challenges.
- **Try to join in with any social activities** that happen within your team. Perhaps the team have lunch together once a month or maybe a colleague is having a leaving celebration. Participating in social activities can help you to get to know colleagues.

> 66 I couldn't have done without my friends from the course – OK you've got your friends at home but they don't really know what you are going through. I couldn't get by without them.
>
> NAS *third-year student*

- **Follow the guidance given to you.** Your university will have provided you with some guidance about the requirements for placement, documents you have to submit and evidence you have to gather. Use it to help you: it has been based on the experience of previous students and aims to help you manage your work.

> **Remember ...** feeling stressed is common. You *can* do something about it.

- **Take care of yourself by planning your working day.** It can be difficult in a busy team but make sure you take regular breaks and at least 30 minutes for lunch. Try to get out of the office and get some fresh air. If you are in a city, try to find a leafy park where the noise levels are lower and the oxygen levels are higher.

Managing your stress

Even if you have followed all the advice given so far, you may still find that your placement is becoming a real challenge and that you are noticing feelings of stress. Don't panic – there are plenty of techniques you can use to make it better, but remember, what will *not* help you is:

- ignoring what is causing you stress and hoping it will go away
- expecting others to solve the problems for you
- keeping your concerns to yourself and becoming more stressed.

There are **three key steps** to managing your stress:

1 identifying what is contributing to your stress
2 changing how you work with the source of the stress
3 managing sources of stress that are hard to change.

Identifying what is contributing to your stress

There will be situations on placement which will be stressful because they are new and demanding. You are learning new skills and being expected to work in a professional environment to meet these demands. Depending on your background, placement may be a very new experience and feeling anxious is a healthy reaction. However, there will always be individual issues so what follows are a few tips for managing stressful placement issues.

Practice issues

- Are you finding it difficult to work with a particular service user?
- Are you unsure about what supervision will be like?
- Is it difficult to understand the agency's IT system?
- Do you not understand what is being asked of you?

Placement issues

- Are you having difficulty settling in?
- Is your practice educator or workplace supervisor not finding enough time for supervision?
- Is the journey to placement long and making it hard to get there on time?
- Are you being asked to accept work that is not appropriate?

Academic issues

- Do you have work from other modules on your course to complete?
- Are you struggling to balance the demands of university and placement work?
- Are you not sure if your tutor will have the time to listen to your concerns?

Home issues

- Is something outside work causing you concerns?
- Perhaps you are feeling guilty about not spending time with your family, partner or friends?
- Is money tight since you stopped work to begin studying?

Exercise 7.1 Stress factors

Write down the things that are making you stressed at the moment and then decide whether they are linked to practice, placement, university or home.

Example: not seeing my children in the evening (home)

Example: having to do uni work while on placement (placement & university)

You ...

-
-
-
-

The key question to ask now is: Can you change how you work with the source of your stress or do you have to 'simply' manage the stress you are under?

Changing how you work with the source of the stress

If you have found out what is causing your stress and think you can change the way you work with this source then read on. Many people find talking through their situation with someone really useful, but who should *you* talk to? Your answer will depend on your situation; see Box A.

Box A | Who should you talk to?	
Practice issue	Talk with your practice educator in supervision, or sooner if necessary. Other colleagues in the office may also be able to help.
Placement issue	Talk with your practice educator in supervision. If you cannot resolve the problem, talk with your university tutor.
Academic issue	Your university tutor or module leader may need to know you are feeling under pressure and so will your practice educator.
Home issue	Talk with your friends and family and, if you can, let a member of the practice learning team know what is going on.

If you have worked out what is causing you difficulties and talked it through with someone, you are taking the right steps to alter the source of your stress. The next step is to **make a plan** (see Exercise 7.2) and change the source of stress into something that is a manageable part of your working week.

Exercise 7.2 Your stress management plan

For one of the stressors identified above, try to make a plan to change the source of stress by using the suggestions below.

Problem

Discussion needed with

Agree action to reduce stress

1

2

3

Who else needs to be involved?

Time scale for change

How will I know it has worked?

Managing sources of stress that are hard to change

Some sources of stress can be dealt with and solved. Others are less likely to disappear quickly. These might include having a heavy workload, undertaking a long journey to placement each day, managing on limited finances and so on. If these aspects of placement cannot be changed or avoided then they need to be managed. So the second aspect of stress management is not changing the source of the stress but learning techniques to manage the stress you experience.

An important way of managing your stress is learning to recognise your own *personal stress signature* – the signs and symptoms that let you know you are starting to become stressed. The idea of a signature best describing the *unique features* of your own experience of becoming unwell originates from research into serious mental health issues (Birchwood 1995). Refer back to the 'What is stress?' section above and remind yourself of the physical, emotional and behavioural changes that might happen if you feel stressed. By writing your own personal stress signature you can personalise your early indicators of stress. For example, rather than looking out for muscle aches you will know that, for you, it is tension in your lower back that alerts you to emerging stress. Like any new skill, writing your own stress signature may take some time to learn and Exercise 7.3 will get you started.

Exercise 7.3 **Knowing your stress signature**

Everyone's stressors are unique, just like your signature, and finding out what raises your stress levels will help you to develop strategies for coping. Below is an example of a social work student's stress signature. Try completing steps 1 to 4 yourself to begin to identify what your stress signature is. Remember, you can use this technique for many different circumstances that you find stressful.

Example: Christine's stress signature

Step 1   What are the triggers for you becoming stressed? *When I'm asked to do too much and I haven't got the time to do it properly. At the moment it is academic work for university as well as my practice work on placement.*
Step 2   What are the early warning signs of you becoming stressed? *I start to feel really restless and agitated, I've no head space to listen to anyone else, and I start to have trouble getting off to sleep. I've also noticed that I start to eat more, drink too much coffee and feel I don't have time to exercise.*
Step 3   What are your ways of coping when you start to get stressed? *I've learnt to stop everything and take a short break, outside in the fresh air if I can, and then sit down and try to decide what it is that is really making me stressed. Is it too much to do, too difficult, not enough time? The answer to this often means I can make a good plan to get things done.* *Sometimes I get some of the easier tasks done – just to get something completed and to feel I'm getting there – and then I focus on the more complicated jobs that need doing.*
Step 4   Who, and what, can help you? *By letting my partner know that I'm feeling stressed and why, it helps him to support me in various ways at home, for example, by keeping the diary free at weekends so I've a bit of time to relax (and get work done). He makes sure there is lots of good healthy food at home.* *What also helps is to remember the times I've had challenges in the past and how I've succeeded in overcoming them. Actively remembering this gives me the confidence to carry on, and to carry on believing that I'll meet this challenge too.*

7

Your stress signature

Step 1	What are the triggers for you becoming stressed?
Step 2	What are the early warning signs of you becoming stressed?
Step 3	What are your ways of coping when you start to get stressed?
Step 4	Who, and what, can help you?

Another way to try to manage your stress is to *check out others' view of the situation*. When you are stressed it can often feel that no one else understands why. However, could it be that if you are stressed you are not viewing some situations accurately? A good way of deciding this is to talk with people whose view you trust to see if they share your perspective on the situation. They may point out that you are being too hard on yourself or be able to suggest ways of coping.

> " I just felt everyone on placement was not interested in me, they didn't seem to want to help and they didn't seem to understand. I talked all this through with my mate from the course who pointed out I was working in a busy duty team, where staff have to respond urgently to calls from A&E. I realised my worries about the placement had made me misinterpret my colleagues' actions.
>
> PHIL *second-year student*

Managing the stress you experience may also include looking after yourself away from placement so that you feel more able to cope with the stress you experience.

You could try:

- ☑ **Relaxing music** – plan periods of relaxation into your day using music to help you.
- ☑ **Time out** – this might include a short break during your working day or may mean taking a day off to rest.
- ☑ **Positive thinking** – it sounds simple and it is! Research suggests that people who think positively and believe they can influence the

world around them are likely to experience lower levels of stress. If thinking positively doesn't come easily to you, then practise. You may soon notice a change in the way you approach situations and how you feel.

Spend some time finding out about and using these different ideas to discover what helps you most to manage your levels of stress.

What if you feel you need extra help?

We hope that, having read this chapter and tried some of the techniques suggested, you are feeling able to look after yourself and manage the stress you experience. However, sometimes it is important to get specialist help if you find that you can't sort out a problem on your own. Do not be afraid of asking for help if you are finding it hard to manage. Asking for help is an effective way to manage your stress; ignoring the problem is not.

7

Who may be able to help?

You may find help from the following:

- **Family and friends.** If it feels right, let them know that you are having some difficulties. They might be able to give some good advice and help you to get further assistance.
- **Practice educator or university tutor.** If you feel able, let them know that you are feeling very stressed and that you may need some additional help. You may want to think about taking some time out of placement to give yourself a break.
- **GP.** S/he will be able to suggest other local resources that could help you, e.g., counselling organisations, and may be able to prescribe some medication (although this is rarely more than a short-term fix). If you need to have medical evidence for your time away from placement your GP will be able to give you this.
- **Local and/or national organisations.** Depending on your situation there maybe an organisation that can help you such as
  - the mental health organisation MIND: www.mind.org.uk
  - nhs direct: www.nhsdirect.nhs.uk

Finally ...

This chapter has focused on how to identify and manage the stress you might experience when you are undertaking your placement. By using the techniques above you can now:

- Take steps to look after your general health to make you more able to cope with stressful situations.
- Identify the physical, emotional and behavioural changes caused by stress.
- Take steps to avoid stress by looking after your basic needs and by creating support networks on placement.

You know that:

- If you can alter the source of your stress this is often the key to reducing the stress you feel.
- The sources of stress can't always be changed and, if this is the case, the management of the source of the stress will be the key to staying well.

Further reading and resources

J. Koch and H. Koch, *Active Steps to Reducing Stress: Life Skills for Feeling Calmer* (Cheltenham: Bracken Books, 2008) provides lots of different techniques for managing day-to-day stress.

R. Templar, *How to get Things Done* (Harlow: Pearson, 2009) is a fun and useful guide to helping you make the most of your time, energy and skills.

www.bbc.co.uk/health has lots of information about coping with everyday life stresses.

www.thesite.org.uk/healthandwellbeing/mentalhealth/anxietyandstress is designed specifically for students, giving a range of information on mental health issues and other student-related topics.

7

8 Troubleshooting

This chapter will help you to ...

- **Explore common difficulties related to practice learning**
- **Cope with challenges as they arise**
- **Problem solve using the CODE model**

---

66 It's important not to be scared to speak up and try to change your situation. You don't have to accept how things are just because you are a student. You actually have to say no to some things. You need to be assertive.

DOMINIC *second-year student*

66 Once I realised how much support I had from my practice educator, I was able to solve some of the difficulties I was having on placement. I came to realise working with service users was a new experience for me and I needed some encouragement and guidance.

JODIE *second-year student*

When you are on placement it is important to remember that you have skills and talents that will help you to succeed. Along the way you may find that you have to work out how to solve some problems that often arise for students on placement. As Jodie indicates, practice learning is a very different experience to academic learning at university and so will present you with different challenges. You have the power to influence and change the course of your placement and overcome the challenges you face.

This chapter will help you to understand how to approach some of the common challenges you may encounter during your periods of practice learning. As Dominic notes, your assertiveness skills will be needed to make sure you find a way through these challenges or make future plans if you think your placement can't continue.

Resolving issues related to practice learning

In the case examples below, we explore some common difficulties experienced by students on placement and suggest ways of trying to move forward. Some of these situations may be close to your own experience, but if not, don't worry; you can apply the CODE model of problem solving (introduced in the following section) to look at options in relation to any other issues that arise on placement.

Team and agency issues

Not enough to do

For example ...

Paul: "I'm on my second placement and I'm just not getting a good enough range of learning opportunities. I'm continually being asked to carry out routine tasks that are usually done by unqualified staff in the agency. They also expect me to spend a lot of time reading files and case records. Surely this isn't real social work? How am I going to get enough evidence to meet the occupational standards and pass the placement?"

Not enough to do: questions to ask yourself	Solutions
Is there a shortage of complex work available in the placement agency?	Discuss in supervision whether a wider range of work could be made available. Revisit the learning agreement which should have documented the learning opportunities that were going to be available. *See:* • 'Taking control of your learning' (Chapter 2) • Exercise 5.1 'Your learning needs in supervision' (Chapter 5)

Not enough to do: questions to ask yourself	Solutions
Does your supervisor lack confidence in your skills?	Discuss the situation in supervision. You could reflect on some work you have already undertaken, incorporating social work theories and knowledge. This will help to demonstrate to your practice educator or supervisor that you are ready for more complex work. See: • Exercise 5.2 'Your existing knowledge and experience' (Chapter 5)
How can the work provide evidence of meeting occupational standards?	Begin producing evidence of your work to discuss with your supervisor. Try to match it to the standards you have to meet – this may not be as difficult as you think. If it doesn't seem to link, highlight the problem to your practice educator. If the issue remains, consider discussing it with your university tutor. See: • Table 6.1 'Considering your evidence' (Chapter 6)

Too much to do

For example ...

Gemma: "I'm feeling really overwhelmed by the pressures on placement. It's bad enough being busy all day rushing from one thing to another but now my friends have started complaining that I can never find time to meet up with them. I feel exhausted all the time, can't face eating and I'm not sleeping well. When was the last time I really chilled out? I'm beginning to wonder if it's all worth it."

Too much to do: questions to ask yourself	Solutions
Is your workload too heavy?	Try to quantify your workload and decide what you think is reasonable to be asked to do. Discuss this in supervision and see if any adjustments can be made. Some students love to be busy; others prefer a different pace of learning. This has a lot to do with learning styles and previous experience. You may need to make sure your supervisor understands how you learn best. Make sure your supervisor knows about other pressures you are under such as caring responsibilities or needing to do part-time, paid work. See: • Exercise 7.1 'Stress factors' & Exercise 7.2 'Your stress management plan' (Chapter 7)

8

Too much to do: questions to ask yourself	Solutions
Is there enough support to stop you feeling overwhelmed?	As a student you will need guidance to help you understand what to do and how to do it. If this does not happen, you may feel overwhelmed due to lack of clarity rather than the *amount* of work. It is important that your supervision sessions have a sufficient focus on support for you. *See*: • Table 5.1 'The four functions of supervision' (Chapter 5)
Are you finding it hard to cope with the emotional demands of social work practice? Are you experiencing unhelpful levels of stress?	Think about where you can go for help and how you might reduce your stress levels. *See*: • Exercise 7.3 'Knowing your stress signature' (Chapter 7)

Lack of support from your practice educator

For example ...

Alex: "My practice educator has been incredibly busy since I started here and has found it really difficult to find time for me. He has cancelled several supervision sessions and every time I need to ask him something I just feel like a nuisance. Now he has gone off sick and it feels like the placement is falling apart around me. How am I going to learn and pass the placement?"

Lack of support: questions to ask yourself	Solutions
Are you receiving the support you need to enable you to meet the standards and pass the placement?	Revisit the placement agreement, which will document the support you should be receiving from the agency and practice educator. Are there back-up arrangements if your practice educator isn't at work? *See*: • 'Your learning agreement' (Chapter 2)
If supervision is being cancelled, is it being rearranged or an alternative put in place?	Is there anyone else in the office who could offer supervision while your practice educator is not at work? Speak to your university tutor. *See*: • Exercise 5.3 'Ground rules' (Chapter 5)
If the placement is really not working, do the placement arrangements need to be renegotiated?	Talk to your practice educator and university tutor about alternative arrangements. Remember, it is the responsibility of the agency, not just the practice educator, to ensure you have sufficient support. It may be quite straightforward to arrange for someone else to take over the practice educator's role but all members of the practice learning team need to be involved and informed.

Not getting on well with your practice educator

For example ...

Tanveer: "I don't like my practice educator. It's not that she's a bad social worker but she just really winds me up – the way she talks, her sense of humour, everything. How am I going to put up with 10 more weeks of this?"

Not getting on well with your educator: questions to ask yourself	Solutions
Is there a particular reason for your feelings? Is this simply a personality clash? Have *you* done enough to try to develop a good relationship with your practice educator?	It helps if you get on well with your practice educator but you can also recognise that you don't need to be great friends to work effectively together. You *do* need to establish a clear professional relationship to meet the aims of the placement. Find ways of acknowledging the practice educator's strengths and build up relationships with others in the team for informal support. *See:* • 'Working together' (Chapter 5)

Different learning style to your practice educator

For example ...

Emily: "I've been on placement for 9 weeks in a friendly, busy team but I just don't seem to see eye to eye with my practice educator. I like to get out there and help people, but Matt seems to go so slow, getting me to read files first and research diagnoses and treatments. Supervision is becoming a nightmare for me – all those awkward questions and silences! I just want to get on with the job."

Learning styles: questions to ask yourself	Solutions
How does your learning style differ from your practice educator? How might this impact on how slowly or quickly you are given work? How might this influence supervision sessions?	Think about how you can use supervision to address your concerns. You could do a learning styles exercise with your practice educator to highlight your different styles. Use this as a basis to discuss how learning styles impacts on all areas of work. Could you use case discussion as a basis for talking about how to apply social work theory? *See:* • 'Models of learning' and Exercise 2.3 'What is your learning style?' (Chapter 2)

8

Feeling that you don't fit into the team

For example ...

Baldev: "The team is just so cosy – all women, all middle-aged, all white. As a black male student, I seem to make some of them feel uneasy – others seem to want to mother me! Whenever they have some work to be done with a black service user it comes to me, even if it's not really going to give me the learning that I need at this stage in my final placement. When I express my views I am always in the minority. I wouldn't exactly call them racist, but they do seem to be treating me in a way which makes me feel distinctly uncomfortable and patronised."

Not fitting in: questions to ask yourself	Solutions
What is actually going on here? Is it a form of racism?	You need to let your practice educator know how you are feeling and that you want colleagues' behaviour towards you to change. If you don't feel you can talk with your practice assessor, contact your university tutor. You or your practice educator may need to ask the team manager to take some action.
How might things change for the better, and is there anything *you* can do to make change happen?	Consider ways of talking to individuals or groups in the team about how you are experiencing their attitudes. Your practice educator or team manager may be able to support you in this.
You need the right support. Do you need to look for this outside the team?	You may find talking to other black and minority ethnic workers, who may have faced similar situations, supportive. Some agencies have black workers' support groups which you might be able to join. Some universities offer black consultants to black students or set up student support groups. *See:* • 'Group supervision' (Chapter 5)
Do you have grounds for a complaint? How might you take this forward and who can best support you in this?	If you conclude you are experiencing discrimination or prejudice you may choose to make a formal complaint. Discrimination is against the professional social work codes of practice and against the law. Consult your university tutor and read your university's guidance about making complaints. Think about who you will get to support you through this process.

Unprofessional behaviour: crossing the boundaries

For example ...

Paul: "There's going to be an important meeting about my future on this placement next week. They found out that I borrowed the pool car for the weekend to visit my brother 300 miles away. Well, it had been loaned to me for an 'out of county' visit on Friday and it was only going to be sitting in the depot all weekend so I couldn't really see what harm it would do. And now they are raking up stuff about my timekeeping and using the internet at lunchtimes to look up holidays."

Ellie: "I have been suspended from my placement. I've been dating this guy, well, a service user I suppose, who I met when I was running a group for parents with disabled children. I mean, he's separated from his wife, but they've reacted as if I've done something really terrible."

Unprofessional behaviour: questions to ask yourself	Solutions
Have you crossed professional boundaries? Do you believe that your behaviour in this situation was reasonable?	Both of the situations quoted would be viewed by placement agencies as seriously stepping over the line of acceptable professional conduct. Your behaviour on placement is viewed as a primary indicator of whether you are a suitable person to be a professional social worker and you need to consider your options in the light of this. Remember what is expected of social workers as set out by the codes of conduct issued by the UK care councils.
	Your developing professional identity will be questioned, but equally not all difficult situations have to end negatively. Depending on the situation, engaging with the process of recognising the identified issues can demonstrate your commitment to learn, and to develop your appreciation of professional standards of conduct.
	If an accusation of professional misconduct has been made, you need to think about whether you feel you have grounds to challenge the accusation, or whether, if it is justified, you should apologise and accept the consequences.
	It may help your situation if you can honestly acknowledge your mistake and show that you understand why it was unacceptable.
	See:
	• Box A 'Who should you talk to?' (Chapter 7)
Consider what support you will need.	If you are in this type of situation you will need to get support from your university tutor during any investigation into your conduct. You may not agree with the allegations regarding your behaviour and you may want to have some form of representation at meetings. This might be a member of the university union, a colleague, family member or solicitor. If you are challenging any complaints or negative descriptions about your conduct, make sure you start to record matters in writing.

8

Unprofessional behaviour: questions to ask yourself	Solutions
What is your response to the outcome or decision? Do you believe that you have been unfairly treated?	You may want to take advice from the student union and study the university handbooks to establish the procedures for appealing against a decision. Legal advice may be also helpful.

University-related issues

For example ...

Helen: "I love my placement but dread the days that I have to go into university. They seem irrelevant, the tutors so out of touch and I'd much rather be getting on with the work on placement."

University issues: questions to ask yourself	Solutions
Is university attendance compulsory?	Attending university during placement time is probably non-negotiable and may form part of your required practice days. You are on a training programme and the tuition available at university is as important as the days on placement.
Why does my placement include university-based days?	Days in university are usually designed to help you meet the occupational standards and make the most of your placement learning. Think about how you can make these days work better for you. Can you bring placement examples to share with fellow students? This may enable you to learn from their ideas and improve your practice. Perhaps you can use the knowledge your tutors have about theory to improve your assessed work on placement. *See*: • 'The importance of theory for social work practice' & Exercise 3.2 'Working with theoretical knowledge' (Chapter 3)

Personal issues and taking time out from placement

For example ...

Steve: "I am feeling really ill and it's getting harder to drag myself to the placement. It seems to be one of those viruses that just go on and on. I'd like a break but I'm worried I won't get one if I don't finish my 100 days before the summer."

Lucy: "I'm a single parent and my little girl has been really ill. They keep sending her home from nursery and there's no one else who can help out with her. Anyway she just wants her mummy. I feel so guilty and I'm not getting much sleep either as she just won't settle."

Mark: "My partner ended our relationship 3 weeks ago. It came out of the blue. He just moved out, no discussion, nothing. I'd thought we were made for each other. I feel awful, totally churned up. My problems are definitely affecting my work. But I daren't take time off."

Personal issues and taking time out: questions to ask yourself	Solutions
Is this manageable stress or do you need to take time out from placement?	Completing your placement is an important goal but sometimes life gets in the way. This may be a situation where you need to put your home and family situation first and take some time out. You won't be working well with service users and colleagues if you have high levels of stress and fatigue resulting from other pressures. Speak to your university tutor. *See:* • Box A 'Who should you talk to? (Chapter 7)
Is there a way you can take a break in a planned way?	Refer to your Practice Learning Agreement to check arrangements for taking time off sick if you are unwell. Talk with your practice educator and university tutor about sick leave or other absences from the placement. Make sure colleagues and service users know that you are taking time out and give an indication of when you'll be back (if possible). *See:* • Exercise 7.2 'Your stress management plan' (Chapter 7)
Do you need to take a longer period away from placement?	You need to consult your university guidance very carefully to see what happens in this situation. Each course has different arrangements and you need to establish whether your placement could be 'put on hold'. You may be able take up the same placement again and complete your work with the agency. Alternatively, you may need to start a new placement when your situation makes it likely you'll be able to successfully complete it. This may have serious implications for other aspects of your study and funding. Check your course guidance and talk with your university tutor in this situation.

8

Problem solving on placement

Problem solving is an important social work skill and you'll have developed your own ways of solving problems through your practice learning. All the examples above, and the suggested solutions, are the start of problem solving. If you are having difficulty on placement, be it similar or different to the examples already given, then it will be useful to have a general model of problem solving that will help you clarify your thoughts and start to make changes. Here we introduce the **CODE** model:

Consider the problem through analysis, defining the problem and reflecting on your situation

Options available to you to change your situation

Decide what action to take

Evaluate the changes made

Use Exercise 8.1 opposite to try out the CODE model. You can use the **CODE** model of problem solving for many of the challenges you will face on placement but occasionally some issues are less straightforward to resolve, and these are considered in the next section.

Unresolved placement issues

Not succeeding on placement

Some students will not be successful in passing their placement. If you find yourself in this position it is worth spending some time trying to understand why, so that you can make well-informed decisions about your next step.

Agency or support issues

Sometimes placement arrangements make it difficult for a student to complete a placement successfully. For example, you may have been given too little work to do or you may not have had enough support and guidance from your practice educator. This might mean you have been unable to demonstrate that you have met the relevant occupational standards. You are entitled to a placement that gives you the opportunity to meet these standards. If you are failing and you think you have not been given a proper chance to show your competence, make sure you keep a clear record of why you believe this to be the case.

Student issues

Life does not stop when you start your social work placement and lots of factors may prevent you successfully completing your placement. You might find it difficult to work with the issues presented by service users, or to cope with the competing pressures on your time between work at the agency, university work and home life. Some students discover that memories of difficult experiences in their own life are awakened by engaging in social work practice and that may make it difficult for them to work effectively. Your expectations of social work practice might have been challenged by your placement. You may conclude that social work is not the career for you.

Use the space below to write down your own placement difficulty and how you can try to solve it using the **CODE** model:

CODE	Your ideas
Consider what you think the problem is	*Try to be specific: who, what, where and when*
Options: what can you do to change your situation?	*Think calmly and seek advice if appropriate*
Decide what action you are going to take	*Make a plan about the actions you are going to take*
Evaluate the changes you've made	*How well have your actions worked out?*

8

As noted in Chapter 6, *Being assessed*, some students aren't able to develop their skills sufficiently to meet the required standard and are unable to complete their studies and enter the profession. As discussed, some students' conduct is unprofessional and unacceptable and in those circumstances universities may use 'suitability procedures' to investigate whether a student should be allowed to continue with their studies.

What happens next?

All social work courses will have procedures that are followed for managing the breakdown, or unsuccessful completion, of a placement.

If you do not think you should have failed your placement, make sure you are aware of your university's appeal procedures. You need to talk with your university tutor about your options, take time to reflect on your future plans and then move forward.

You may have to attend meetings with your practice educator and university tutor to ensure everyone has a shared understanding of why the placement has not been a success. If you have further evidence of how your work on placement meets the relevant occupational standards, or if you believe that the evidence you have already presented has not

> **Remember ...**
> social work is not the right career for everyone. If you do decide it's not for you, this is not a *personal* failure.

been taken seriously, make sure these factors are highlighted in any correspondence or meetings.

As with any course of study, not all students pass every element first time and it is often possible to retake practice placements, just as you are often able to resubmit academic work. Engaging with the process of resolving your placement issues may feel difficult and stressful, but ultimately if you are a student who has the essential ability to survive their placement then behaving appropriately and professionally will serve to demonstrate to those around you your suitability to continue with your training. It will also stand you in good stead for the difficult situations, involving working and negotiating with others, that you will encounter in practice.

Finally ...

This chapter has helped you to think about how you can use your skills and knowledge to overcome the challenges you may face on placement.

If you are experiencing difficulties:

- Use the experiences described here to help you to make links with your practice.
- Try out the **CODE** model. It will help you to find a way to meet the unique challenges you are facing.
- Remember that most students successfully pass their social work placements and all of these students will have had challenges, like the ones you will face, along the way.

9 Moving on from your placement

This chapter will help you to ...

- **Plan and achieve positive endings**
- **Assess your professional development**
- **Return to university**
- **Prepare for your first social work job**

"I didn't really think about the end of my placement until it came. It just sort of happened. I wasn't really prepared for it and I wasn't prepared for going back to university either.

YASMIN *first-year student*

"By my final placement I'd learnt quite a bit about endings and how important it was to finish things properly for me and for the people I was working with.

EVE *third-year student*

9

Social workers know that endings and transitions can be times of great significance in their practice with service users and carers. Similarly, reaching the end of your placement and moving on to whatever comes next represents an important point in your life as well as in your social work training. In this final chapter we will help you find positive ways of managing the end of your placement. With careful planning, you can use this final phase to consolidate your learning and skills and prepare yourself for the continuation of your training or for the beginning of your social work career.

Planning and achieving positive endings

Moving on

Whether you are reaching the end of a placement that is part-way through your social work training, or finishing a final placement, you will be in the process of developing as a practitioner. The ability to critically reflect on your practice, as you have been encouraged to do throughout this book, is essential to the development of your professional identity and something you should continue to do throughout your career. Even if you are not yet at the end of your training, you are on the road to becoming a professional practitioner and this aim should remain central to your next steps.

One element of social work theory you may have learnt about is issues relating to loss and transitions. It is useful to reflect on how these ideas may impact on your thoughts and feelings as you come to the end of your placement, and affect how you manage the process of moving on to the next stage of your professional life.

Coping with mixed emotions

Reaching the end of your placement will probably leave you with all sorts of feelings and emotions. These can sometimes be contradictory and confusing. Past students have described all the feelings below and many more besides:

relief   disappointment   ambivalence

loss   fear   sadness

pride   happiness   elation

If you are one of the small numbers of students whose placement ends unhappily and whose experiences we looked at in Chapter 8, *Troubleshooting*, you will of course feel differently from those students who have enjoyed their placement. For most, however, the ending of a placement is characterised by both pride *and* relief; loss *and* elation. In other words: mixed feelings are completely normal and to be expected.

There are, nevertheless, ways of making sure that your placement finishes in the most positive way possible *for you*. An important dimension is to make sure that the several endings it involves are well planned. By doing this you should be able to avoid the common experience described by Yasmin at the beginning of the chapter, of an ending which 'just sort of happened' and over which she seemed to have no real control. The section below will help you to think about positive endings in relation to some key groups and individuals. There may, of course, be others you need to consider, depending on your particular placement:

☑ Service users and carers
☑ Your practice educator
☑ Your team(s)
☑ Yourself

Positive endings: service users and carers

As a future professional social worker, your first responsibility is to service users and carers. Ensuring that those you are working with are fully prepared for the fact that you are leaving is an important aspect of this – something Eve, who is quoted at the beginning of the chapter, realised by her final placement.

The most appropriate ways of ending your contact with service users and saying goodbye will depend on your particular placement. If you have been placed in a setting where your work is inevitably short term, such as

Remember ... it's important to think about and plan endings, right from the beginning of placement.

a hospital Accident and Emergency department, your contact with service users will have been brief. In situations like this, ending relationships will probably be a skill you have learnt and consolidated throughout your placement, rather than something which comes mainly at the end. On the other hand, if your placement is somewhere like a residential setting with a group of adults or children with learning difficulties, you will need to give careful thought, well in advance, to the best way of preparing those you are working with for your departure. Exercise 9.1 on the following page might help you think about ways to do this.

You can read more about ways of understanding and gathering feedback on your practice from service users and carers in Chapter 4, *Keeping service users central to your learning and practice*.

Positive endings: your practice educator

There will probably be one person who has been more closely involved than anyone else in your learning and in assessing your practice through the course of your placement. How you feel about saying goodbye to this individual will of course depend on the relationship you have had during the placement. In the case of practice educators, it will probably also depend on whether you have passed the placement and what sort of feedback you have received. In some settings, there may have been a number of people involved in your supervision and assessment, in which case you will need to think about how you end your relationship with each of them.

The responsibility for making sure that your relationship with your practice educator ends in

9

The examples below worked for these students in their placements, but you can probably think of other approaches that might work well for you in your particular setting. Use the space at the bottom of the chart to plan your own endings with service users and carers.

Placement setting	When? What? Why?
Julie was on placement in a small residential centre for children with behavioural and emotional difficulties	"My practice educator explained the importance of talking to the children right from the beginning about the fact that I was a student and that I would be leaving the centre before most of them. We used it as a way of talking about moving on and the children made me cards and presents when I left."
Li was on placement in a community team for disabled adults	"I was working quite intensively with a couple of older people and their carers. I was hoping to finish the work before I left, but it just wasn't possible. My practice educator made arrangements well in advance for someone else to take over after I left, so we were able to do two joint visits and have a transition period before I finished. One of the carers wrote a really nice letter, thanking me for my help and wishing me luck with the rest of my studies. I think it was important for her to feel involved in the end of my placement."
Your placement ...	

a way that is positive for both of you should be a shared task. There are, however, several things you can do to play an active part in ensuring this. Exercise 9.2 offers some suggestions. As in the previous exercise, you can adapt it and add ideas, according to the structure and context of your particular placement.

Remember ... placement can feel like a rollercoaster. If you can take some control over the ending, it will help you to feel positive about the whole experience.

Plan in advance

Think about ...

The importance of successfully planning the end of your placement is as relevant to your relationship with your practice educator and other colleagues as with service users and carers.

There will be lots to talk to your practice educator about before you finish your placement, from arranging the handover of work to the assessment of your own practice and ongoing professional development. Try to ensure that meeting times are planned in both of your diaries well before your actual finishing date.

What will *you* do to make sure this happens?

Receiving feedback/ final assessment

Think about ...

Consider the dialogue you have had with your practice educator during your placement and how you have discussed the work you have undertaken in supervision. Receiving feedback at the end of your placement should be the natural continuation of this ongoing dialogue.

You can play your part in ensuring that this happens, by actively seeking feedback throughout and particularly towards the end of your placement. It is unlikely that all the feedback you receive will be positive. This is a **good** thing. The most confident and competent social work practitioners are those who are aware of their professional development needs and understand the importance of continually seeking to improve their practice.

What will *you* do to make sure this happens?

9

Giving feedback to your practice educator

Some things to think about ...

The ending of your relationship with your practice educator is a two-way process. Many practice educators will ask you for feedback on the part they have played in your learning, but if they don't, this is something you might want to suggest. You may be asked by your college or university to complete a form commenting on your placement experience, but it is probably more powerful and effective if you can give your feedback face to face. The ease or difficulty of this will depend very much on your placement experience, but giving a full and honest response can be a helpful way of ending a difficult or challenging placement as well as a pleasurable way of finishing a placement you have enjoyed.

What will *you* do to make sure this happens?

Cards, gifts and saying 'thank you'

Some things to think about ...

Some students choose to give a card or gift or perhaps to write a letter of thanks to their practice educator. After all, supervising and assessing social work students can be a demanding and time-consuming activity, for which practitioners often get little workload relief! Whether or not you choose to do this will depend on your personal style, your relationship with your practice educator and on the culture of the team in which you are based. Either way it is worth spending some time thinking about the most appropriate way to personally acknowledge the contribution and commitment of your practice educator.

What will *you* do to make sure this happens?

When things don't go to plan

If your placement breaks down or ends in some other way you would not have chosen, you may be left feeling that your relationship with your practice educator has become difficult or even antagonistic (see Chapter 8, *Troubleshooting*). In situations like this, trying to end the placement positively will be even more important. Ensuring that you mark the end of your relationship with your practice educator and, if possible, acknowledge each other's point of view, will help you to move on from the experience in as positive a way as you can.

Positive endings: the team

The way in which the ending of your placement is marked by the wider team will probably depend more on team culture and the setting of your placement than on how well they feel it has gone. If a friend of yours on placement in a different team gets a bigger send-off than you, it isn't because they are more popular or more successful.

Just like the ending of your relationship with service users and with your practice educator, the ending of your relationship with the team will probably feel more satisfactory if you are proactive and plan it in advance. Some things to consider are:

- **Formal and informal feedback**
  You may want team members to give you feedback about how well they think you have done on placement. It is important to be clear about whether this is part of your assessment to be included in an assignment or portfolio, or whether it is informal feedback for your own information and development. Busy colleagues

will appreciate being given a clear and reasonable time scale, particularly for formal written feedback you might request.

- **Saying goodbye**
  If yours is the sort of team that socialises together outside work, the end of your placement may be marked by a drink or some other social event. If this is the case, don't forget to also say goodbye to administrative staff or others who may not be involved in this. Alternatively, you might want to thank the whole team at a team meeting or some other workplace gathering. You could discuss when and where would be appropriate with your practice educator or with the team manager.

- **Letters and cards**
  Some students also send a card or letter of thanks to the team. If you do this, allowing yourself time to think about what you really want to say will leave you (and them) feeling more satisfied with the ending of the placement, than a few last-minute words.

Positive endings: yourself

Everything we have thought about so far in connection with endings involves *you* in relation to other people. However, it is also important to spend time thinking about what the end of your placement means for you specifically. Much of the rest of the chapter is concerned with your *professional* development and the ways in which you might carry your learning back to university or into the workplace. It is also worth taking time to consider the *personal* impact your placement has had and what this will mean for you in the future. It would be inappropriate for us to suggest what this might be or how you should manage it, but the experiences of the students quoted below might help you to reflect on the personal impact of your own placement and what this means for you.

> My placement was hard on my family. I felt like I was asking a lot of my partner and my kids. I love social work, but I'm thinking of working part time when I qualify.
>
> PHIL *second-year student*

> My placement brought into focus something I guess I already knew about myself – that I don't find it easy to be among new people. I'm never going to be the person who walks into a group and immediately makes friends, but being aware of that has helped me find strategies for coping.
>
> EVE *third-year student*

> I discovered that I'm a lot stronger than I thought I was! My second placement was quite tough, but I really surprised myself by achieving things I didn't imagine I was capable of.
>
> JODIE *second-year student*

> I feel I'm a different person now. Social work training makes you think about what you believe in and what your priorities are and for me, my first placement was a turning point. I suppose I could say my personal values have changed.
>
> ELLEN *second-year student*

Assessing your professional development

As a social work student, you are at a beginning point in your professional development and you will go on learning for the rest of your career. The end of a placement is a helpful point at which to summarise the level of your competence and confidence in relation to particular practice activities in order to create an Action Plan for the future (see Exercise 9.3).

This exercise asks you to 'self-assess' your practice skills on a scale of 1–10 and then to create an action plan for your future development. We have listed two examples of knowledge and skills for practice to get you started, but you will be able to think of many more. You can use the blank charts below to begin this process.

Practice knowledge/skill: *Group work*	**Self-assessment rating** 1 → 2 → 3 → 4 → 5 → 6 → 7 → 8 → 9 → 10 No experience or knowledge Very confident about my knowledge and experience

ACTION PLAN
What will you do to further your development in this area?

1 _____

2 _____

3 _____

Practice knowledge/skill: *Applying theory to practice*	**Self-assessment rating** 1 → 2 → 3 → 4 → 5 → 6 → 7 → 8 → 9 → 10 No experience or knowledge Very confident about my knowledge and experience

ACTION PLAN
What will you do to further your development in this area?

1 _____

2 _____

3 _____

9

Practice knowledge/skill:	Self-assessment rating
_____ _____ _____	1 ⟶ 2 ⟶ 3 ⟶ 4 ⟶ 5 ⟶ 6 ⟶ 7 ⟶ 8 ⟶ 9 ⟶ 10 No experience or knowledge Very confident about my knowledge and experience

ACTION PLAN
What will you do to further your development in this area?

1 _____

_____

2 _____

_____

3 _____

_____

Practice knowledge/skill:	Self-assessment rating
_____ _____ _____	1 ⟶ 2 ⟶ 3 ⟶ 4 ⟶ 5 ⟶ 6 ⟶ 7 ⟶ 8 ⟶ 9 ⟶ 10 No experience or knowledge Very confident about my knowledge and experience

ACTION PLAN
What will you do to further your development in this area?

1 _____

_____

2 _____

_____

3 _____

_____

Professional development plan

Exercise 9.3 will be particularly useful if you are asked to write a 'professional development' or 'learning' plan. It is likely that whether you are now at the end of your social work training or whether you are moving on to the next stage or level, you will be expected to consider your learning so far and to think about the areas you need to develop in the future.

In Chapter 2, *Learning for practice*, you were given tools to help you consider your strengths and learning needs at the beginning of your placement. By the end of your placement, you will have a wide range of new learning on which to reflect so it may be helpful to go back to the advice in Chapter 2 in the light of this. It is essential to be honest with yourself during the process of reviewing your learning. While it is important to celebrate your strengths and newly acquired areas of competence, it is also necessary to be honest about the gaps in your knowledge and the areas you need to develop in the future.

> **Remember ...**
> the more *aware* you are of your learning, the more you will be able to use it.

Returning to university

If you have been doing a 'block' placement, where all or most of your time has been spent away from university, it may feel quite strange to go back and to have to readjust to the rhythm of being a full-time student. Your response to this change will depend very much on you. You may feel excited about the opportunity to apply your new practice experience to your academic work or you may be itching to finish your course and get back to practice. Either way, it is important for your development as a competent professional social work practitioner to make the most of the next period of academic learning, just as it was important to make the most of your practice learning on placement.

Unlike taught academic modules or courses, your placement is a unique experience – it is something which only happened to you and not with a room full of fellow students. This means that you are the only person who can make the links between your practice and your academic learning and you need to be *proactive* about doing this.

Box A provides a simple illustration of the interaction between the theoretical knowledge that you might associate most closely with academic learning and the practice knowledge that you probably associate with your placement. The important message here is the interrelationship between the two, which *together* form the basis of the knowledge you need to be a really effective social worker.

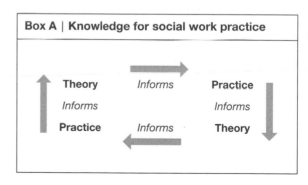

Box A | Knowledge for social work practice

Theory — *Informs* → Practice
Informs ↑   ↓ *Informs*
Practice ← *Informs* — Theory

Preparing for your first social work job

If this was your final placement, it may be your stepping stone into the world of qualified social work practice. Many exciting challenges await you, not least the next steps in your professional training.

At this stage you may not feel you will ever want to do another training course! However, as you continue to develop your practice as a social worker, you will realise that there is always more to learn. Your continuing professional development is key to ensuring that service users work with someone who has continued to improve their knowledge and skills for practice.

How you feel about applying for your first professional social work job, your priorities and preferences and the degree of urgency with which you approach this, will depend on your individual circumstances.

The availability of qualified social work posts is also subject to many variables, including agency funding, location, time of year and availability of qualified practitioners. It is therefore important to maintain a sense of control over the application process. Your first social work job is a significant stage in your development towards becoming a more competent practitioner, so time taken to consider your priorities will be well spent. You may find it useful to list these priorities by identifying the aspects of any potential post that you regard as *essential* and *desirable*. It may be that your *essential* list has to include practical considerations such as

location or hours of work, but it is also important to think about areas of practice that you know you do not want to take on at this stage and those you definitely want to be part of your first job. Use the list to jot down those aspects you consider essential and desirable to *you*.

Essential
1
2
3
Desirable
1
2
3

It is important to remember that many of the things employers will be looking for are closely related to the ideas and activities we have asked you to think about in this book. For example:

- Using supervision effectively
- Keeping service users central to your practice
- Understanding your learning and professional development needs
- Applying theoretical knowledge to practice
- Being able to manage stress

These are all areas you can usefully return to as you complete job application forms and attend interviews. Similarly, the skills you have developed in critical reflection and analysis can be used very effectively in the process of applying for jobs. Make use of the tools you have been given in this book and elsewhere during your training, to reflect on your skills and knowledge in relation to particular posts. This will help you to create an impressive application and prepare well for interview. If you are unsuccessful at first, the same process of reflection will help you to think about what you can learn from the experience and how you might improve your performance next time.

Finally ...

We hope that this book has helped to enhance your learning and make your placement a positive experience. There will almost certainly have been things that went well and things that didn't go so well. Our aim has been to provide you with ways of making good use of the challenges as well as helping you to celebrate the successes. Whether you are now returning to college or university for further study or entering the world of professional practice, we wish you every success and enjoyment in your social work career.

Further reading and resources

R. Adams, L. Dominelli and M. Payne (eds), *Social Work – Themes, Issues and Critical Debates*, 3rd edition (Basingstoke: Palgrave Macmillan, 2009). Joyce Lishman's chapter, 'Personal and Professional Development', encourages reflection on your professional development as a social worker.

Remember to check out the websites of the relevant care councils to make sure you are aware of what is required, in terms of registration and professional development, once you complete your training:

England: www.gscc.org.uk
Wales: www.ccwales.org.uk
Scotland: www.sssc.uk.com
Northern Ireland: www.niscc.info

Appendix A:
National occupational standards for social work
(England, Wales and Northern Ireland)

Key Role 1	**Prepare for, and work with individuals, families, carers, groups and communities to assess their needs and circumstances** Units: 1 Prepare for social work contact and involvement 2 Work with individuals, families, groups and communities to help them make informed decisions 3 Assess needs and options to recommend a course of action
Key Role 2	**Plan, carry out, review and evaluate social work practice with individuals, families, carers, groups, communities and other professionals** Units: 1 Respond to crisis situations 2 Interact with individuals, families, groups and communities to achieve change and development and to improve life opportunities 3 Prepare, produce and implement and evaluate plans with individuals, families, carers, groups, communities and professional colleagues 4 Support the development of networks to meet assessed needs and planned outcomes 5 Work with groups to promote individual growth, development and independence 6 Address behaviour which presents a risk to individuals, families, carers, groups and communities
Key Role 3	**Support individuals to represent their needs, views and circumstances** Units: 1 Advocate with and on behalf of individuals, families, groups and communities 2 Prepare for and participate in decision-making forums

Key Role 4	**Manage risk to individuals, families, carers, groups, communities, self and colleagues**
	Units:
	1 Assess and manage risk to individuals, families, groups and communities
	2 Assess, minimise and manage risk to self and colleagues
Key Role 5	**Manage and be accountable, with supervision and support, for your own social work practice within your organisation**
	Units:
	1 Manage and be accountable for your own work
	2 Contribute to the management of resources and services
	3 Manage, present and share records and reports
	4 Work within multi-disciplinary and multi-organisational teams, networks and systems
Key Role 6	**Demonstrate professional competence in social work practice**
	Units:
	1 Research, analyse, evaluate and use current knowledge of best social work practice
	2 Work within agreed standards of social work practice and ensure own professional development
	3 Manage complex ethical issues, dilemmas and conflicts
	4 Contribute to the promotion of best social work practice

Reproduced with permission of Skills for Care and Development

The complete National Occupational Standards for England, Wales and Northern Island are available via the care councils' websites:

www.gscc.org.uk
www.ccwales.org.uk
www.niscc.info

Appendix B:
Standards in social work education
(Scotland)

Standard 1	**Prepare for, and work with individuals, families, carers, groups and communities to assess their needs and circumstances**
	Learning focus:
	• Preparing for social work contact and involvement
	• Working with individuals, families, groups and communities so they can make informed decisions
	• Assessing needs and options in order to recommend a course of action
Standard 2	**Plan, carry out, review and evaluate social work practice with individuals, families, carers, groups, communities and other professionals**
	Learning focus:
	• Identifying and responding to crisis situations
	• Working with individuals, families, groups and communities to achieve change, promote dignity, realise potential and improve life opportunities
	• Producing, implementing and evaluating plans with individuals, families, carers, groups, communities and professional colleagues
	• Developing networks to meet assessed needs and planned outcomes
	• Working with groups to promote choice and independent living
	• Tackling behaviour which presents a risk to individuals, families, carers, groups, communities and the wider public
Standard 3	**Assess and manage risk to individuals, families, carers, groups, communities, self and colleagues**
	Learning focus:
	• Assessing and managing risks to individuals, families, carers, groups and communities
	• Assessing and managing risks to self and colleagues

B

Standard 4	**Demonstrate professional competence in social work practice**
	Learning focus:
	• Evaluating and using up-to-date knowledge of, and research into, social work practice
	• Working within agreed standards of social work practice
	• Understanding and managing complex ethical issues, dilemmas and conflicts
	• Promoting best social work practice, adapting positively to change
Standard 5	**Manage and be accountable, with supervision and support, for your own social work practice within your organisation**
	Learning focus:
	• Managing one's own work in an accountable way and contributing to the management of resources and services
	• Taking responsibility for one's own continuing professional development
	• Contributing to the management of resources and services
	• Managing, presenting and sharing records and reports
	• Preparing for, and taking part in, decision-making forums
	• Working effectively with professionals within integrated, multi-disciplinary and other service settings
Standard 6	**Support individuals to represent and manage their needs, views and circumstances**
	Learning focus:
	• Representing in partnership with, and on behalf of, individuals, families, carers, groups and communities to help them achieve and maintain greater independence

Reproduced with permission of the Scottish Executive and Scottish Government

The complete Standards in Social Work Education for Scotland are available from the Scottish Social Care Council's website:

www.sssc.uk.com

References

1 Getting started

Durkheim, E. (1983) *Pragmatism and Sociology*. Cambridge: Cambridge University Press.
Trevithick, P. (2005) *Social Work Skills – A Practice Handbook*. Buckingham: Open University Press.
Twelvetrees, A. (2002) *Community Work*. Basingstoke: Palgrave Macmillan.

2 Learning for practice

Beverley, A. and Worsley, A. (2007) *Learning and Teaching in Social Work Practice*. Basingstoke: Palgrave Macmillan.
Fook, J. (1996) *The Reflective Researcher*. St Leonards: Allen & Unwin.
Fook, J. (2002) *Social Work: Critical Theory and Practice*. London: Sage.
Fook, J. and Gardner, F. (2007) *Practising Critical Reflection: A Resource Handbook*. Maidstone: Open University Press.
Gibbs, G. (1988) *Learning by Doing: A Guide to Teaching and Learning Methods*. Oxford: Further Education Unit, Oxford Brookes University.
Honey, A. and Mumford, P. (1986) *A Manual of Learning Styles*. Maidenhead: Peter Honey Publications.
Howe, D. (2009) *A Brief Introduction to Social Work Theory*. Basingstoke: Palgrave Macmillan.
Kolb, D. A. (1984) *Experiential Learning: Experience as the Source of Learning and Development*. New Jersey: Prentice Hall.
Race, P. (1993) *Never Mind the Teaching – Feel the Learning*. SEDA Paper No. 80. Birmingham: SEDA Publications.
Race, P. (1995) *Making Learning Happen*. London: Sage.
Schön, D. (1983) *The Reflective Practitioner: How Professionals Think in Action*. London: Temple Smith.

3 Using theory and knowledge in practice

Beckett, C. (2006) *Essential Theory for Social Work Practice*. London: Sage.

British Association of Social Workers (BASW) (2002) *The Code of Practice for Social Workers*. Birmingham: BASW.

General Social Care Council (GSCC) (2002) *Code of Practice for Social Care Workers*. London: GSCC. www.gscc.org.uk (accessed 4 February 2009)

International Federation of Social Workers (IFSW) and International Association of Schools of Social Work (IASSW) (2004) *Ethics in Social Work, Statement of Principles*. Berne: IFSW and IASSW. http://www.ifsw.org/en/p38000324.html (accessed 4 February 2009)

Sheldon, B. (1995) *Cognitive Behavioural Therapy: Research, Practice and Philosophy*. London: Routledge.

Topss/Skills for Care (2002) *National Occupational Standards for Social Work*. Leeds: Topss.

Trevithick, P. (2005) *Social Work Skills: A Practice Handbook*. Maidenhead: Open University Press.

4 Keeping service users central to your learning and practice

Arnstein, S. (1969) 'A Ladder of Citizen Participation', *Journal of the American Institute of Planners*, 35 (4) (July), 216–24.

Beresford, P. and Croft, S. (2004) 'Service Users and Practitioners Reunited: The Key Component for Social Work Reform', *British Journal of Social Work*, 34, 53–68.

Boylan, J. and Dalrymple, J. (2009) *Understanding Advocacy for Children and Young People*. Maidenhead: Open University Press.

DoH (Department of Health) (2002) *Requirements for Social Work Training*. London: Department of Health.

Franklin, B. (ed.) (2002) *The New Handbook of Children's Rights: Comparative Policy and Practice*, 2nd edition. London: Routledge.

General Social Care Council (GSCC) (2002) *Code of Practice for Social Care Workers*. London: GSCC.

John, M. (ed.) (1996) *Children in Our Charge: The Child's Right to Resources*. London: Jessica Kingsley.

Laming, W. (2003) *The Laming Report into the Death of Victoria Climbié*. London: The Stationery Office.

Shier, H. (2001) 'Pathways to Participation', *Children and Society*, 15, 107.

Taylor, P. and Dalrymple, J. (2005) 'The Hub and Spoke Model'. Unpublished paper.

5 Making the most of supervision

Hawkins, P. and Shohet, R. (2007) *Supervision in the Helping Professions*, 3rd edition. Buckingham: Open University Press.

6 Being assessed

The Care Council for Wales, Raising Standards (2004) *The Qualification for the Degree in Social Work in Wales* [online] at: http://www.ccwales.org.uk/eng/training/pdf/raising_standards.pdf (accessed 30 March 2009)

COSLA, QAA for Higher Education, Scottish Social Services Council and Scottish Executive (2003) *The Framework for Social Work Education in Scotland* [online] at: http://www.scotland.gov.uk/Resource/Doc/47021/0025613.pdf (accessed 30 March 2009)

Doel, M. and Shardlow, S. M. (2005) *Modern Social Work Practice: Teaching and Learning in Practice Settings*. Aldershot: Ashgate.

Northern Ireland Social Care Council (2003) *The National Occupational Standards for Social Work* [online] at: http://www.niscc.info/content/uploads/downloads/workforce_dev/NOS_socwork/SocWork_NOS_Jan2003.pdf (accessed 30 March 2009)

Parker, J. (2004) *Effective Practice in Social Work*. Exeter: Learning Matters.

Topss UK Partnership (2004) *The National Occupational Standards for Social Work*, May 2002. Leeds: Topss.

7 Managing stress on placement

Birchwood, M. (1995) 'Early Intervention In Psychotic Relapse: Cognitive Approaches to Detection and Management', *Behaviour Change*, 12, 2–19.

Cottrell, S. (2007) *The Exam Skills Handbook*. Basingstoke: Palgrave Macmillan.

9 Moving on from your placement

Lymbery, M. (2005) 'Loss and Transition in Relation to Older People', in *Social Work with Older People: Context, Policy and Practice*. London: Sage.

Index